A-Z OF

MANAGEMENT FOR

HEALTHCARE

PROFESSIONALS

A tool-kit for management in times of change, pressure, mayhem,
tension, demand, necessity, urgency, problem, puzzle, doubt,
disbelief, hesitancy, perplexity, dilemma, jam, pickle, plight,
predicament, circumstances, contingency, situation and every day!

Roy Lilley

Radcliffe Medical Press

Radcliffe Medical Press Ltd
18 Marcham Road
Abingdon
Oxon OX14 1AA
United Kingdom

www.radcliffe-oxford.com
The Radcliffe Medical Press electronic catalogue and online
ordering facility.
Direct sales to anywhere in the world.

British Library Cataloguing in Publication Data

A catalogue record for this book is available from the British Library.

ISBN 1 85775 953 2

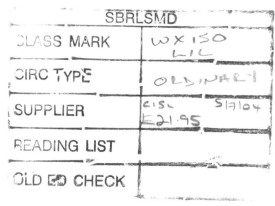
Typeset by Advance Typesetting Ltd, Oxfordshire
Printed and bound by TJ International Ltd, Padstow, Cornwall

PREFACE

AN A–Z OF MANAGEMENT FOR HEALTHCARE PROFESSIONALS

What's that all about?

First, make a note. If you think you have bought a book about the A–Z of management, you haven't. Ask for your money back. This is not *the* A–Z of Management. It is *an* A–Z of Management. There's a difference.

What I mean is, the 26 words that take us through this alphabet of management are my choice, highly subjective, personal to me and idiosyncratic! Would you expect anything else?

As I wend my way up and down the UK, across Europe and the US, talking to managers, looking at organisations, poking a stick through the bars and having fun, some common themes emerge.

Pressure, tension, demand, deadlines, resources, stress – they are all there. For everyone. Not just in the overburdened public services. They are common themes in the private sector and voluntary organisations. Big business and small business. In the boardroom and at the coalface.

These are tough times. Managers are under increasing pressure to perform. Benchmarking, lists, comparisons. You will be familiar with all that. One thing is for sure, it isn't going away.

So, how do you become a five star manager, do well, get promoted and double your salary? Don't ask me! The questions are probably more about hanging on to your job, paying the mortgage, and survival!

What I can tell is that the 26 words that I have chosen for my alphabet are all words that encapsulate and describe a management style or achievement, or perhaps habits or routines, that have impressed me. They are obsessions and addictions that have marked someone out for success. They are words that describe the extra 'thing' that made a manager stand out, sparkle, seem different from the rest.

Roy Lilley
July 2002

GETTING THE BEST FROM THIS BOOK

The first thing to do is not to read the book. By that I mean, not from cover to cover. That's very dull. Have a flip through the pages, scribble a few notes in the margin, fold the pages over, rip bits out. That's all fine.

Get the feel of it.

Make a coffee and flip through the pages because I want you to decide how to use the book to suit you, to get the best advantage from it.

You'll see there are several icons:

'Think boxes' are there to *get the juices flowing* and to get you thinking *outside the box* – look at the issues from a different dimension. Some are deliberately provocative; some just for fun.

Hazard warnings are there to point out some tricky issues; bear traps for the unwary – or those without the wisdom to have bought this book.

The tips are short cuts and quick fixes to get you to the answer faster.

The exercises are there for you to address the issues in the context of where you work and what your task is – regardless of your profession or seniority in the organisation. Use them to develop your own thinking or for brain-storming the issues with colleagues.

Done that? Good. Now, we need to talk...

How are you going to use the book? There are several ways:

- Put it on the shelf in your office, along with all the other management guru books, and impress people with your library.
- Leave it lying around so that people can see that you've made a bit of an effort at self-development.
- Give it to someone else in the hope of looking wise and helpful.
- Use it to hit subordinates on the head.
- Throw it at colleagues who are driving you barmy.

Or...recognise there are 26 ideas and you could:

- Focus on one idea a day and get through the book in just under a month (if you are sad enough to read it on Saturdays and Sundays).
- Focus on one idea a day and get through the book in just over a month (if you are not sad enough to read it on Saturdays and Sundays).
- Take just over two years, if you focus on one idea a month.

The whole point of this is to use the words to inspire some thinking, personal development or other reading from a proper management book.

Either way, make a plan. Decide how you want to get the best from the book and stick to it. Read it on the train, at lunchtime, before you drop into the arms of Morpheus, or whilst at your ablutions.

The idea is to make this book one of those books that eventually gets read from cover to cover, dog-eared, and inspires you into some sort of action, movement, activity, energy, response, change, rage, satisfaction – anything. Really, anything will do. Doing nothing is not an option.

I've made it as easy as I can for you – a bit at a time.

American management guru Tom Peters talks of undertaking a task. He asks the question: 'If the task seems like it is the size of an elephant, think: how would you eat an elephant?'

His answer is: 'Elephant stew, elephant kebab, elephant rissoles, elephant burgers...' In other words, a bit at a time.

There's an old saying. Here it is. Rip it out of the book, stick it onto the fridge door with a funny magnet thing, tape it to the dashboard of a car, pin it on the notice board.

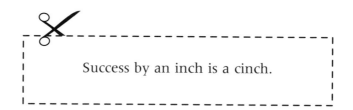

Success by an inch is a cinch.

So, don't turn this book into an indigestible mess. Take it a letter at a time, think about what it means to you, your task, where you work, what you are doing now. Ask yourself if it makes sense, can it help, is there something more to do? If not, move on. Getting better at what you do shouldn't be a chore. Have fun.

The more *you* progress, the better we *all* do.

One final thing – they are only words. And, we all know, actions speak louder than words.

Nobody plans to fail, they just fail to plan.

So make a plan.

I plan to visit this book:	Check
Daily	
Weekly	
Monthly	

Letter	Daily	Weekly	Monthly	Done
A				
B				
C				
D				
E				
F				

Letter	Daily	Weekly	Monthly	Done
G				
H				
I				
J				
K				
L				
M				
N				
O				
P				
Q				
R				
S				
T				
U				
V				
W				
X				
Y				
Z				

ACKNOWLEDGEMENT

Throughout the book I've sprinkled some great quotes. I hope they make you think and laugh as much as they did me!

They were collected and passed to me by:

The Regional Finance Staff Development Team,
Training Schemes Office,
North Bristol NHS Trust.

– who says finance people have no sense of humour! – via:

Philip Gray,
Penyard Press,
Studio Two,
Parkfields Gallery,
Pontshill,
Ross-on-Wye
HR9 5TH

Tel: 01989 750553
Fax: 01989 750553
info@penyardpress.com

Thank you!

For ATR who, as well as understanding my alphabet,
has my number!

...and Benjamin, who is yet to struggle with the alphabet
but who is getting to grips with the lexicon of life!

Any good strategy will seem ridiculous by the time
it's implemented!

Dogbert's Rule of Strategies

ASSERTIVE

assertive adj. *1 tending to assert oneself, forthright, positive 2 dogmatic*

What a start! I could have begun with amorous, or articulate, or even, when push comes to shove, aspirin. No, I thought about this carefully. Appealing, apologetic and attentive are all very well. So is aphrodisiac. But it is not the right word.

Assertive is a very good word to start with and is an attribute that many managers lack. That's why they are stuck being junior or middle managers.

Top managers are always assertive. They are dogmatic in their beliefs but not bossy or a bully. Being assertive means being forthright and is part of those indefinable qualities that good leaders have.

They are the kind of people 'you know where you are with'. They are positive. They can make up their mind.

Being assertive is also about standing up for what you want. I've come across a huge number of great middle managers, stuck in a career groove, simply because they are not assertive.

Assertive can mean rude, abrupt, difficult and all the negative things. But it can also mean some good things, too. It might mean confrontation – and that means courage – dealing with a boss or a colleague who is a bully. Remember, bullies need a victim and assertive people are seldom victims.

All my experience tells me assertive people:

- manage colleagues and their personal lives more effectively
- are able to say 'no' and enjoy a more balanced lifestyle, because they know what they want
- increase their work effectiveness and productivity because they are usually more positive and able to manage their time better
- feel more in control of their daily activities and are usually less stressed.

How do you see assertiveness?

- Getting your own way?
- Forcing others to do what you want?
- Seeing your needs as more important than anyone else's?

How about...

> The belief that we all have needs to be met and that we all
> have rights.

Needs? What's that all about?

There are some management gurus that we can turn to for some advice. It will also give you some names to drop and make you look really cool at the next management meeting. For example, one such is the celebrated Maslow.

Maslow's theory of motivation tells us about a hierarchy of needs which have to be met. These range from our basic physiological needs through to needs of recognition and self-fulfilment.

The other name you need to drop is Hertzberg.

Hertzberg's theory describes key motivators as:

- achievement
- recognition
- work
- responsibility
- advancement.

Hertzberg also gets a bit depressed and describes de-motivators. They are:

- salary
- company policies
- status
- security
- personal life
- relationships with peers, bosses and subordinates.

So, where does assertiveness fit into all this? For a start, it is about being able to achieve Hertzberg's key motivators. Can you be an achiever, have recognition, do the work you want to do, accept responsibility and obtain advancement without being assertive? I doubt it.

What about trying for a decent salary, influencing company policy, having achievements, obtaining status and security, making time for a personal life and getting on with the people you work with, without being assertive? Never.

 See, there's more to assertive than aggressive.
The belief that we all have needs to be met and that we all have rights.

OK, that's *needs* taken care of, what about *rights*? Management gurus talk about *assertive rights*. In summary, they usually end up with a list something like this.

You have the right to:

- judge your own behaviour, thoughts and emotions, and to take responsibility for their consequences
- offer no reasons or excuses for justifying your behaviour
- judge if you are responsible for finding solutions to other people's problems
- change your mind
- make mistakes but be responsible for them
- say 'I don't know'
- be independent of the goodwill of others before coping with them
- be illogical in making decisions
- say 'I don't understand'
- say 'I don't care'

...and you have the right to say 'no' without feeling guilty.

 Hazard Warning

I'm not too sure that some of these 'rights' wouldn't be a bit career-limiting in some of the places I've looked at. Nevertheless, if you are a boss, even a mini-boss, it would be nice to think that you could create a working environment where these sorts of rights were respected. Wouldn't it?

Perhaps there is another way of putting it. A guru couple (can you imagine the conversations over the breakfast table?), Ken and Kate Black, in a neat book, *Assertiveness at Work* (McGraw-Hill, London 1992), have another way of looking at this. They say...

You have the right to:

- know what is expected of you
- know how your manager sees your performance
- get on with the job in your own way once objectives and constraints have been agreed
- make mistakes from time to time
- expect work of a certain standard from your staff
- criticise the performance of staff when it falls below the required standard
- be consulted about decisions that affect you
- take decisions about matters that affect your department or area of work
- refuse unreasonable requests.

Tell me you can achieve all that without being assertive!

 Maybe we're making this too difficult. Aren't we just talking honesty here?

Couldn't we sum this up as:

- expressing yourself in a clear, affirmative manner
- helping others around you grow by giving direct, honest feedback
- knowing about yourself and your career ambitions
- being productive
- getting your message across without stepping on others' toes.

✍ Ask yourself, have you ever:	Yup	Never
• felt you are being manipulated or exploited by your boss/relative/friend?		
• felt dissatisfied with your social life?		
• felt guilty saying 'No' even to an unreasonable demand/request?		
• been afraid to speak up?		
• felt defensive even though you were unjustifiably criticised?		

If you can honestly tick *Never* for all of these, you should go on to the next chapter and see what **B** stands for!

However, if you have a few *Yups*, ask yourself: how did you deal with it? Passively? Aggressively? Be honest!

Either passive or aggressive means there is a row brewing. Passive people explode – eventually. Aggressive people explode all the time. What about assertive people?

Try an assertiveness inventory. Think about how you can:

- develop assertive behaviour for better personal and professional life
- be more aware of your rights
- express your feelings, wants, and ideas more effectively
- develop a more positive self-image
- handle unfair demands, conflicts and discipline problems effectively
- say 'no', mean it and not feel bad about it
- avoid being exploited or manipulated
- be confident and positive when speaking up.

What are your training needs?

Here are some simple techniques. Try them:

THREE STEPS TO ASSERTIVENESS

	Check ✔
1 Make sure you understand and summarise the facts of the situation	
2 Be clear that you can indicate your feelings towards the situation	
3 Think through and be ready to state your requirements, reasons and how it will be good for the other party	

In plain English, fill out the blanks:

1 'When you ....' (*state facts*)
2 'I feel uncomfortable ....' (*say what you feel*)

3 'I would like .... (*state requirements*) ....; then we will be able
   to work together more productively because ....' (*benefits to the
   other party*)

See? Assertive is not about being rude. It is about being, well, er, assertive!
   Got the idea? Here are some other things to try:

• Be honest with yourself about your own feelings.
• Talk to yourself! Rehearse in your mind and be ready to be positive. Tell
  yourself you *can* do, *can* achieve, *can* deal with this or that.
• Be clear, specific and direct in what you say.
• If you run into a brick wall or a tide of objections, just stick to the facts, be
  assertive and repeat your message. Don't be put off.
• If there is uncertainty, ask for the facts, for clarification.
• Respect the 'rights' of everyone else.
• ...And keep cool, calm and collected!

So, now you know, all you have to do is practice. But first, try this:

 Exercise

Think about some typical situations where a little assertiveness might
just do the trick. How about appraising a member of staff, saying 'no' to
extra work (even a camel can get a broken back) and asking someone for
help?

   Try some role-play with a colleague. Generate a scenario about a poor
performing person, an in-tray that is the size of the Eiffel Tower, or one of
the awkward squad you need to ask for help:

1 Explain the situation.
2 Use role-play to talk through the situation. Make your points clearly
   and get the other person to respond as the appropriate character.
3 Ask the other person what you did well and what you could improve.
4 Finally, swap roles, so you can swap ideas and see the situation from
   the other person's point of view.

 Well done! Take a break and go on to the **B** section tomorrow, next
week or next month. Whatever your plan says.

The function of leadership is to produce more leaders, not more followers.

Ralph Nader

BRAG

brag v.&n. *1 talk boastfully **2** boast about **3** a card game, like poker*

Right, let's be clear about this. Forget the cards! And I'm not talking bragga-docio or braggart here. A braggadocio (great word, isn't it?) is someone given to empty boasting, unlike a braggart who, justified or not, does it all the time. No, forget that.

I'm talking about letting people know how good you are, being upfront about your achievements and your experiences. Too many managers get passed over for promotion or preferment because they are too shy to talk about the great things they've achieved.

There's something about the British. We can't seem to celebrate success. Do well, buy a nice car, park it and be certain to come back and find a big scrape down the side of it. Be successful in the USA and buy a nice car, park it in the street and expect to come back and find a crowd around it. They'll be admiring it and telling each other how soon they will 'have one just like it'.

So, bragging? We're talking strategic bragging. Planned boasting and targeted flaunting! Why not? If you've got it, flaunt it. And that's the first message. Make sure you have something to brag about! We all have something to brag about. Nine times out of ten, we just forget what it is.

 Tip

Be like the character in Gilbert and Sullivan's *Mikado* and 'have a little list'. At the back of your note book, diary (if you still have a paper pile – ugh!), personal organiser or in a secret place, keep a list of things you have learned, skills you have developed and good pieces of work. Add to it every week, without fail. Come appraisal time you'll have something to talk about, a lever to use for promotion and the basis for freshening up your CV.

Dealt with a really difficult situation on the phone? Make a note of it. It is a bona fide achievement. Sorted out a sticky problem with a customer or staff? Make a note of it, it is a 24-carat accomplishment. Solved a problem, delivered the impossible, jumped tall buildings in a single stride? Write it down. Why not? It is a copper-bottomed piece of career insurance. You are good at something!

Done a stunning proposal, a Powerpoint presentation to die for, a report in record time? Keep a copy and put it into your appraisal file or attach an anonymised version to the paperwork when you go for your next job.

You are good – very good – but sometimes you need help remembering. If you don't remember, if you don't brag a little, no one will do it for you.

What about your staff?

Find some reasons for bragging about them. Let them hear you say things like: *'I couldn't have done it without this great team of people.'*

Brag about an individual: *'We're really lucky to have Amanda working with us. She's done us proud with this project.'*

Thinking about going for a new job? This takes some careful bragging! Time to turn bragging into a fine art...

YOUR CV, BRAGGING AND YOU

How's your CV? Where's your CV? On a disk somewhere? Down the back of the armchair? In the bottom of the parrot's cage?

You should:

- know where it is
- have a list of things to add to it
- be able to update it, pronto.

 Tip

Get your head around the idea that there is no such thing as a 'CV'. Really? Yup. Think of a CV as an introduction to you. If you were in a room of people you might well introduce yourself differently to different people. Older people, younger people, people whose first language is not English. It is the same with a CV. You will need the same basic information but presented differently for different circumstances.

An internal CV for internal promotion. A CV that emphasises your people management skills for a people job and your planning skills for a

---

planning job. Horses for courses – get the idea? As you change, so does the CV. Think of your CV as a tool to help you achieve what you want. Sometimes you need a hammer, other times a screwdriver.

Here are the basics of a CV that brags, boasts and brings you into the limelight without anyone realising.

THE SECRETS OF THE STEALTH CV

It is a good bet you are not the only person to be sending a CV for a job interview, promotion or whatever. So, first impressions count. You've got ten seconds to impress and get yourself filed in the 'must see' pile and avoid the 'dump this lot' pile. If there are 100+ applicants (and there often are) you have to be the *one-in-a-hundred*.

How do you do that? Easy. Sell your best stuff on the front page. Just like a shop window. In other words match your experience to the job advert and get it on the leading page. Put your personal or educational details, your out-of-work hobbies and all the other junk at the back.

At this stage it is all about getting an interview. You need a short list of your capabilities and a list of your major, stunning achievements – enough to make the selection person say: 'Wow, I must meet this star, they are a match made in heaven.'

Choose a layout that grabs them by the eyeballs. Plenty of white space (like this book), easy to read, with headings and section breaks that jump off the page.

 ## Hazard Warning

Use a word-processing package and stay away from desktop publishing. If you've got fancy lines, 300 typefaces, drop shadows, boxes, clip art and embossing tools, you'll be tempted to use them. They will look horrible, amateur, immature and naff. Got the picture? Oh, and use good quality A4 paper, preferably 100g, for both your CV and covering letter. Not coloured paper, paper recycled from the hair of the armpit of a Tzumistan mountain goat, nor the pretty stuff with the flowers on.

How long?

Two pages. Yup, two pages of careful, thoughtful well chosen words. Yes, I know you have a million qualifications, experience up to the eyeballs and are an all round dish of the day. But, unless you are asked for something in detail, two pages is enough. Your prospective new boss doesn't want your life history – they just want to know if you are worth time, interviewing.

Get organised

- Use paragraph headings as signposts and bullet points as markers. Keep sentences and paragraphs short and punchy.
- Include some stuff on where you are working now and the job you are doing. Make it relevant to the post you are seeking.
- You need to brag about your achievements. This is your sales leaflet and must tell the prospective, sceptical new boss why they should invest in you. How are you going to show them a return? Sell them your benefits.
- Die, rather than send in a CV with misspellings or poor grammar. You will look sloppy, thick and casual. So, use the good old spellchecker and if you are not sure, get a friend to read your CV through. Look for typo's and mstkes. (They are easy to miss!)

 Should you use a professional CV service?

Big job, lot riding on it, make or break? Well a professional CV is a possibility. Have a look on the Internet and you'll find ten thousand companies who offer a service. Some are real swish outfits and some are former managers who have set up shop in the back bedroom.

If you have a particular career problem a pro CV writer might be a good idea. They will want to know everything about you and everything about the prospective job. This will take time.

Be clear what their fees are. Some of the companies are part of job agencies or headhunting firms and use the CV-writing offer as a come-on to find prospective employees for their client base of prospective employers.

You'll need to spend some time harvesting information. Here are the basics:

- your full name, address, home telephone number
- date of birth (not age)

- marital status (divorced? Use 'single'. Separated? Then you are still 'married'. Never, never, never list any type of failure on a CV. Don't use 'divorced' even if you were the tragically wronged, innocent party. You would say that, wouldn't you?)
- nationality (this is really if you are applying for jobs abroad or if you are a British/EU national and your name does not sound British)
- driving licence details (if it is clean, say so. If not, say nothing. Remember – nothing negative).

EDUCASHUN

- List your qualifications in reverse chronological order (latest first).
- List your professional qualifications, membership of professional associations, and if you are a member of a profession that has a register, include your ID number.
- If you have completed a college or university degree or HND or Diploma, etc, list the courses you studied if your subjects were relevant to the job.

Don't forget any training courses you've been on. Include internal company courses and any evening classes or distance learning you have done in your own time. Don't leave out charity work. If it is smack-on-the-nose relevant, put it in the 'jobs' section. If not, bung it into the 'interests' section.

MIND THE GAP

Got a gap in your chronology? A period unemployed? This makes prospective employers think of prison, illness, time in detox and just about everything else bad. Have a good reason for a gap and get it down on paper.

Start with your most recent or last job and work backwards. For each position (Been promoted? Present that as a new job and show the dates separately):

- list your job title (e.g. Manager, Supervisor, etc)
- show the job title of the person you reported to (e.g. Director, Manager, etc) – this underlines your seniority
- give start and finish dates of all jobs
- spell out what you did, along with the main responsibilities
- list your skills, responsibilities, achievements and duties. *Match them to the job you are looking for.*

 Tip

Be positive about your skills and use words that 'sell' them. Good written skills, excellent people skills, wide experience with customer complaints. Sell, sell, sell!

- Impress with your level of responsibility. 'Managed a department with a budget of £200K with 15 staff.'
- Increased productivity/savings/revenue? Say so and quantify it. Say by how much, include volumes and numbers.

Time to brag, with style and skill and cunning.

WHAT ARE YOUR ACHIEVEMENTS?

Yup, I know you've done it all, been there and got the T-shirt. However, don't go over the top. Think about what you've done. Pick the four or five achievements that most fit the specification of the job you are after. Major on them. You can list all the other amazing stuff, later in the CV. Target what they are looking for in a candidate, with what you have done.

WHAT ELSE CAN YOU DO?

Make a list:

- Computing skills you have and stuff you can make work: PC, Mac, Microsoft Windows 95, Microsoft Office 97, Windows NT, Office Pro, Windows ME, Windows 2000, Excel, PowerPoint, Access, Windows XP and all that sort of thing.
- Speak a foreign language? Très bon! Say so. Indicate the level: spoken, written, business or technical, restaurant, nightclub, pillow talk! Fluent? Good working knowledge, familiar, rusty. Be honest and don't get caught out.
- What else? Keep it relevant, please.

OUT OF WORK INTERESTS?

Sports, hobbies, run a boys club, do meals-on-wheels, organise a charity? Brag a little and show what a nice, warm, community-minded person you are.

 References

Don't include them on the initial CV, but think about who you will approach and ask them, in advance, to support you. Some professions will want to take up references before interviewing you.

What gets left out is as important as what goes in.
   Don't include:

- Some CV gurus will say 'no photographs'. They argue that, while you may think you are lovely and no doubt your mother does, too, unless you are applying for a role in the next James Bond movie (or perhaps airline cabin crew), leave it out. I'm not so sure. If you have a nice passport-photo size picture that makes you look businesslike, gorgeous and lovely, why not include it? Don't use holiday snaps or pictures that are in any way technically or presentationally dodgy.
- Had something go pear-shaped? Job, relationship? Don't mention it. Remember, nothing negative.
- Reasons for leaving previous jobs? Leave them out but be prepared to be asked at interview.
- Previous salary information. They might ask later. Just assume that you are worth what they are offering (and more)!

...And don't use:

- title pages, binders and folders
- if you are a science whiz who has published loadsa papers, sorry; now is not the time to list them
- photocopies that are obviously photocopies – it makes it look like you are in the *give-us-a-job* hunt. In any case, your CV should be tailored and targeted for each specific job.

OK, so what does a super, get-the-job CV look like? Here's an example.
   The bits in **bold** are the sign-posts for you to follow. Use them to make a perfect fit with the job advert or specification.

Jennifer Williams
108 The Ridings,
Birminghurst M99 1QQ
Tel: (0199) 987 654

PROFILE:

- A Senior Administration Manager, **widely experienced** in the widget industry. **Able to** work as part of a team and alone. **Proven** leadership skills focused on managing, developing and motivating teams and people **with the aim** of meeting targets and objectives. **Experienced in** people skills and budget management. **Dedicated to developing and maintaining** high quality standards and customer liaison.

MAJOR ACHIEVEMENTS:

- **Introduced** a new administration system that identified late order delivery and saved the company £150K in lost orders.
- **Implemented** a new computer-based stock control system, on time and within budget.
- **Achieved** Investors in People accreditation for a department of 30, since rolled out company-wide.
- **Solved** customer liaison difficulties with staff not based centrally.

EXPERIENCE:

1992 – date	**Whizzo Ltd**
	Senior Administration Manager Whizzo make widgets under the brand name Whizzget in a state-of-the-art factory in Brimwell.
	Responsibilities and achievements: • **Managed** all administration for sales and commercial activity. • **Reported** directly to the Admin Director. • **Responsible for** a team of 30 people; planning their work, agreeing objectives, and encouraging them to meet corporate targets. • **Demonstrated** the quality assurance admin procedures to prospective customers on visits to the factory. • **Performed** audits of Investors in People procedures.

1985 – 1989	**Terriffoo plc**
1986 – 1989	**Administration Assistant** Terriffoo plc manufacture a wide range of engineering products. **Responsibilities:** • **Developed** new internal admin systems to speed payment and collection of customer accounts. • **Tested** new computer systems. • **Conducted a survey** of customer attitudes to the company.
1985 –1986	**Junior Administrator** **Worked** in the wages department. **Responsibilities:** • Collected information from new and existing staff, to pay tax and wages. • **Solved and fixed** any problems other staff had with their use of the IT system.

TRAINING:

Various courses including: Quality Assurance, The Investors in People Quality Approach, Team Leadership NVQ parts 1 & 2, Time Management (evening class), Report Writing in MS Excel and Word.

QUALIFICATIONS:

• **BSc. (Hons) 2.1** in Business Administration at the University of Mancinham (1984)
• **4 A Levels:** English [B], Maths [A], Biology [B], Chemistry [C]
• **5 O Levels**

PERSONAL DETAILS:

• Date of Birth: 23rd June 1963
• Marital Status: Single
• Driving Licence: Full, clean

INTERESTS:

Aerobics, cycling and voluntary service with meals on wheels.

Is this for you?

Some recruitment gurus suggest you open your CV with a short 'mission statement'. The idea is to encapsulate 'you', your vision, experience and aspirations in 30 or so words.

Feel comfortable with that? Give it a try and see how you end up.

Make a list of your talents, skills and aspirations. Think about your main strengths, attitudes and the direction in which you want to go. Ask yourself the question: 'Where do I want to be in five years' time?'

You might find it easier to discuss them with a partner or close friend. Work on it together.

You should end up with something that looks like this:

A qualified management professional able to lead and motivate others, aiming to achieve senior management responsibility in the developing area of web-based services.

Now you try:

A qualified .... able to ...., aiming to achieve

.... in the *developing* area of ....

Comfortable with that? Good. Stick it at the front – brag a little!

FINALLY, FINALLY. . .

Make every word count. Remember, you are selling you! Use words like:

> delivered, operated, consolidated, administered, evaluated, negotiated, accomplished, achieved, initiated, generated, pioneered, purchased, demonstrated, increased, created, planned and promoted.

Every word you use should be screened to check that it's positive rather than passive.

Make sure that your wonderful CV arrives on the desk of the inquisitor unfolded, stapled in the top left-hand corner only, and uncrumpled. Invest in a hardback envelope.

 Tip

Make sure your name and contact number are on every page of the CV – put it in the footer. Don't know how to do that?

Open Microsoft Word. From the menu bar, select View | Header and Footer, toggle between header and footer, and type in your details. Align them centrally and click on Close. Easy!

E-MAIL APPLICATIONS

In this whizzo world the old snail-mail is taking a bashing. Increasingly you're going to be e-mailing your CV to prospective employers.

There are some traps.

- If you send your CV in the main body of an e-mail, it might change format when opened by the recipient.
- If you send your CV as an attachment, you might find out, too late, that the company has a policy of deleting all e-mails with attachments because of the risk of viruses.

Try attaching a note indicating which program your CV should be opened in. Call up and find out in advance what they want you to do. When all else fails, there is always snail-mail!

Need a covering letter? Do this:

- Address your letter to the correct, named person within the firm and be sure to check all the spelling, names and so on.
- Type (I mean word process) the addresses and body copy and top and tail the salutation and sign-off by hand. Use 'Dear Mr Big-Bloggs' and end 'Yours sincerely'. Forget 'Dear Sir' and 'Yours faithfully'.
- If you're responding to a job advert, give the full title of the position, mention where you saw the ad', and give the appropriate reference number at the top.

Your letter should look something like this.

Dear Mr Brown – *in your own hand*

REF: 2001/6/78/ Locality Manager

   Further to your recent advertisement in The Gronidad, I am writing to apply for the above position.

   I am a public service professional and a self-motivated team player and leader. I have demonstrated my ability to work within budget and have an in-depth understanding of current good practice and legislation.

   I enclose my CV and ask, please, to be given the opportunity to attend for interview.

Yours sincerely

Gladys Snoods

That's it, good luck! Brag a little and have a look at **C**.

All assignments are eventually delegated to the person who understands them the least!

Dogbert's Theory of Delegation

C

CONFIDENCE

confidence n. *1 firm trust 2 a feeling of reliance or certainty 3 a sense of self-reliance, boldness*

How's your confidence? We're not talking parachuting out of an aeroplane or walking a tightrope over the Amazon. Just ordinary, everyday confidence. Confidence in meetings, the confidence to stand up in front of a group and make a presentation. Confidence to talk to the public on a phone, strangers in a crowded room or confidence to stand up for yourself.

What is it about confident people? They have a sort of aura, don't they? You can spot a confident person. Not smart people, or bumptious people or big-headed people. Just the kind of people who always seem to know what they're doing.

Are they different? Confident people do seem able to face challenges, maybe take a risk. Confident managers do get the job done and motivate their staff better. They seem willing to leave the comfort zone of inactivity and try new things. Leaders seem able to instil confidence in the people around them.

How's it done? Is there a trick? Not really. But there are, like all skills, techniques to learn and practice to be had.

And don't forget, people can lose their confidence. After a serious accident, or a bad personal experience, some folk see their confidence go down the drain. As a manager you will be interested in your own confidence and building the confidence of those around you.

CONFIDENCE BUILDERS

Four simple steps:

- Tell people! Simple really. If you want someone to act confident, then tell them you have confidence in them. If you have a member of staff handling a tricky situation, say: *'I know you think this is difficult but I am confident that you can handle this.'* Talking to staff facing a challenge for the first time, say: *'I know you can do this. I've seen the way you handle yourselves and I am totally confident you will pull this off.'*

- And when they do come through with the project, the deal, the result – use it as a confidence builder: *'Well done! I told you I was confident you could do it and you have proved me right. Congratulations, a great job!'*
- The more competent people are, the more confident they are. What improves competence? Training and practice. Build your and other people's confidence by investing in training and personal development.
- Empowerment. In other words, describe the task, make sure the resources are in place and transfer the ownership and responsibility down the line. Real leaders give real responsibility and real authority. They are rewarded by people who know they are trusted and behave conscientiously and with confidence. Real leaders know they are trusted.
- Give someone the confidence to succeed by reminding them of their previous successes. They did a good job on one project, so they can do a good job on another. Maybe you know they have had a success in a non-work related arena, maybe a sport or hobby. What does that bring to the workplace and how does that improve their self-confidence?

The next four points are leadership actions. Getting the best out of people by affirming your confidence, recognising their accomplishments, skilling and training them, letting them get on with the job and reminding them of previous successes.

Are we born with confidence or can we make it, find it, acquire it or be trained?

Helping people to be more confident is part of the management coaching role. Yes, we can train staff (and ourselves) to be more confident.

TRY THE 'LOOK, SHOW, ASK, GIVE' TECHNIQUE

LOOK

Look at people carefully. How do they behave? How are they when they stand up in front of a group of people? Do they handle meetings well? Do they speak to the public easily? Look for what self-development gurus call 'teachable moments'. Find the moment when they are most susceptible to learning. When they have done a good presentation, give them another one to do. When they know they haven't done so well, use the opportunity to say: 'I could see you tried really hard to get that right. Shall we work on some techniques to make it better next time?'

SHOW

Show them what great performance looks like. If you can do something well, show your people, give them an example to copy. Encourage them to watch and learn from the best in the business.

ASK

Develop the questions that will help people face and energise them. 'How do you think you did?' 'What do you think were the best bits?' 'What do we need to do now?'

GIVE

Give feedback. Be candid, fair and sensitive. Do it regularly and use it to celebrate progress. Show that you are confident in their ability to learn and grow from every experience.

...And you? Set the example. Demonstrate your confidence by seeking feedback and opportunities to get even better at what you do.

THE FAST TRACK TO GREATER CONFIDENCE

If you want to feel good, then just – feel good!

Faced with something that dents your confidence? Asking yourself 'Why did I let myself in for this?' Time to make yourself feel good. Think of three things that make you feel good. A memory, a person, a place, some music, an achievement, a photograph, a holiday. Anything. As long as it makes you feel good. Gurus in the art of self-motivation teach this. Apparently the way the brain-box works: 'emotions attach themselves to memories'. Practice thinking about the good things and your confidence to do other things will build.

Feeling self-conscious? Then stop thinking about 'the self' – in other words, you! If you start to feel anxious about you, start thinking about something other than you. Look around the room. Think about the wall decoration, the pictures, who painted them. The carpet, who put it down.

Think about colours, textures, shades. Focus on anything but you. Feeling self-conscious in a group? Focus on the group and doing something. Get the drinks, start a conversation, ask someone a question, swap business cards. Keep the brain-box distracted!

Don't put up with unreasonable criticism – even from you! Just bear in mind: even the most confident people have their bad moments! And, just because you feel like death, everyone is looking at you and your confidence level is zero – no one else is going to notice and even fewer will care. They are all worrying about their own problems!

Feel like you're no good at anything? Stop telling yourself that. Anyway, it's a stupid lie. Everyone is good at something. Don't let yourself make sweeping statements – they can really screw up your self-esteem. Good self-esteem is not about thinking good stuff about yourself – it's all about not thinking bad stuff!

Felt bad in the past? That's no reason to feel bad now. The past is the past – draw a line in the sand. (Now where did that come from?)

✎ Exercise

Make a list of the good memories that you plan to distract yourself with.

1
2
3
4
5
6
7
8
9
10

Pick the favourite three and remember to practice remembering them!

1
2
3

Are you ready for **D**, yet? Where are you in your alphabet plan?

As we look ahead into the next century,
leaders will be those who empower others.

Bill Gates

D

DIFFICULT

difficult adj. *1 needing much effort or skill **2** troublesome, perplexing*

Difficult what? Difficult decisions? Difficult report? Difficult budgets? No, let's do difficult people!

People, difficult people, that's the one we seem to have the most trouble with.

Here are a few tips.

Make a start by cutting this out, sticking it on the fridge door with one of those magnet things and reminding yourself every day.

Dealing with difficult people

The first rule:
There is no such thing as a difficult person, there are just people we need to learn how to deal with…

The second rule:
Re-read the first rule…

And whilst you are about it, cut this out, too.

The six most important words:	'I admit, I made a mistake.'
The five most important words:	'You did a good job.'
The four most important words:	'What is your opinion?'
The three most important words:	'Would you mind?'
The two most important words:	'Thank you.'
The one most important word:	'We'
The least important word:	'I'

If our car won't start it's no good blaming the car. No good kicking the tyres, shouting at it and slamming the doors. Maybe it needs petrol, a service, a new battery. Who knows what it could be? We just find out what the problem is and fix it.

The same logic applies to people. If we have difficulties with our families, colleagues we work with, or our friends, what's the point of blaming them? Figure out the reason and then fix it.

DIFFICULT? MOI?

Yes you! Before you can think about dealing with difficult people, let's start with you. Are you difficult? Are you the one out of step? Are you the one with the problem?

Here's some bad news for you: nice people are not always like you! Yes, yes, I know the world would be a much simpler place if everyone was like you, but they're not. They will have different backgrounds, different education, different perspectives, different cultures and different ambitions. They will be motivated differently and think differently. And they can still be nice people!

So the number one rule in dealing with difficult people is:

Don't take it personally!

OK, so what do you do? Easy. Ask yourself this question:

> What do I want to get out of this encounter?

Decide, in advance:

- What is your purpose?
- What are the key results you want to achieve?

 **Hazard Warning**

Really difficult people are most likely to be selfish and inwardly focused. They won't give a toss about you. For them – it's all about them. So, don't let them get under your skin!

Then, ask yourself:

> Do I need to change MY behaviour to get the most out of it?

This doesn't mean you have to let a rude pig trample all over you. But it does mean you don't need to get into a bare knuckle fight.

Think about it!

The brutal truth is, they don't care about you...

This may come as something of a shock, but there aren't too many people out there that care too much about you. There's your Mum, she probably still loves you, family, partners and a few friends, maybe. But, when push comes to shove, you're on your own.

How we treat each other is largely a product of how we feel about each other. Most folk start off neutral, we don't feel anything about each other. You might be lucky and find a pre-prejudiced soul who is downright antagonistic, but the fact is most people couldn't care less about you.

What do they care about? Answer: they care about themselves. They, are into them, in a big way. That's why they're difficult.

What can you do about it? The brutal truth? Not much! It is very unlikely that you will change them. Anyway, why bother? There is a much easier way.

Remember this:

Difficult people are predictable people.

That simple fact makes your life much easier. How many times have you heard folk say: *'Oh, don't bother with him, he's a misery'* or *'Don't ask her, she finds fault in everything.'*

You see, difficult people are not just difficult with you. They are into themselves and are, usually, difficult with everyone. Predictable is easy. You can prepare for difficult, you can plan for difficult, you can plot, scheme and collude against difficult. They are stuck in their ways. All you have to do is to be smart enough to manoeuvre.

This doesn't mean becoming a soft touch, or a pushover. It means you use your brains more than your emotions. The trick is to decide in advance what you want out of an encounter, plan accordingly and go for it.

If you know someone is a nit-picker and a stickler for detail – give them detail. 'In the report I've included all the background I can think of, including spreadsheets for four scenarios. Let me know if there's something else you need.'

If someone is abrupt, get straight to the point, avoid flannel and go to the heart of the matter. 'I know you are very busy so I'll come straight to the point. What do you think about this next phase of the development?'

If someone is an egomaniac – tell 'em how good they are. 'Jane, I know you are the neighbourhood expert on this, so I've put the detail together and made a couple of recommendations. But, can I leave it to you to come up with some alternative directions, if you think they might be better?'

The strategy is easy. You won't change a difficult person by being difficult. By deciding what you want out of the encounter and being prepared to manoeuvre, trim, side-step, change, call it what you like, you end up winning. You end up getting what you want!

> It's so easy that you will end up wishing everyone was difficult – because the difficult ones are easiest to manage!

Don't think difficult people are predictable? Let me tell you, difficult people are so predictable that behavioural psychologists and other management guru experts reckon there are just seven classic types.

A number of psychologists have come up with definitions and metaphors for the seven types. I think the best work comes from a big brain-box of someone called Robert Bramson. He did the work in 1988.

Bramson starts by identifying aggressive people and uses a neat metaphor to describe them. Really, they almost explain themselves. Bramson tells us aggressive people divide into three sub-types:

- the Sherman Tank
- the Sniper
- the Exploder.

Here's Bramson's advice about the Sherman Tank:

> The term Sherman Tank accurately depicts what a hostile person does. They come out charging. They are abusive, abrupt, intimidating, and overwhelming. They attack individual behaviours and personal characteristics. They bombard you with unrelenting criticisms and arguments. Sherman Tanks usually achieve their short-run objectives, but at the cost of lost friendships and long-term erosions of relationships.
>
> Sherman Tanks have a strong need to prove to themselves and others that their view of the world is right. They have a strong sense of how others should act, and they are not afraid to tell them about it.
>
> Sherman Tanks value aggressiveness and confidence. This belief causes them to devalue individuals they perceive as not having those qualities.

> The basic core belief of a Sherman Tank is, 'if I can make you out to be weak, faltering, or equivocal, then I will seem, to myself and others, strong and sure.'

The Sniper?

> Snipers prefer a more covert approach. They put up a front of friendliness behind which they attack with pot shots, use innuendoes, non-playful teasing and not so subtle digs. Snipers use social constraints to create a protected place from which to strike out at objects of anger or envy.
>
> They pair their verbal missiles with non-verbal signals of playfulness and friendship. This creates a situation where any retaliation back at the Sniper can be seen as an aggressive act, like you are doing the attacking not the defending.
>
> Much like the Sherman Tank, Snipers believe that making others look bad makes them look good. They also have a strong sense of what others should be doing, but their constant cutting remarks usually de-motivate colleagues rather than produce results.

And the Exploder? Exploders are characterised by fits of rage fuelling attacks that seem barely under control. Bramson says:

> These tantrums can erupt out of conversations and discussions that seem to start friendly. Usually these tantrums occur when the Exploder feels physically or psychologically threatened. In most cases an Exploder's response to a threatening remark is first anger followed by either blaming or suspicion.

Who's next?

THE COMPLAINERS

Complainers moan like hell about everything but never seem to take any action to change anything. It is almost as if they like having something to moan about. Complainers are not the individuals who have legitimate complaints and a desire to find a solution to the problem. The Complainer is someone who finds fault in everything. Sometimes they do have a real complaint, but rarely do they want to find a way to fix the problem.

Here's what the guru Bramson said about them:

> The constant complaints can cause people around the Com-
> plainer to feel defensive.
>   Complainers view themselves as powerless, prescriptive, and
> perfect. These beliefs cause Complainers to convert useful prob-
> lem solving into complaining. Their feeling of powerlessness
> causes them to think that they cannot change things so they had
> better complain to people who can.
>   Their prescriptive attitude gives them a strong sense for how
> things ought to be and any deviation from that produces com-
> plaints. Complaints are a way for the Complainer to confirm that
> they are not in control or responsible for things that are done
> wrong, reaffirming perfectionism.

THE SILENT UNRESPONSIVE

A silent, unresponsive person deals with any disagreeable situation by shut-
ting down. Ask them what they think and you'll be rewarded with a grunt!
(Bit like a teenage son!)
    Let's turn to the work of another management psychologist and
organisation dynamics guru, Lewis-Ford, who wrote in 1993:

> The Unresponsive use silence as their defensive weapon, to
> avoid revealing themselves, so they can avoid reprimand. *[Just
> like a teenage son!]* On the other hand, it can be used as an aggres-
> sive, offensive device, as a way to hurt you by denying access.
> An unresponsive person in some cases might be distrusting of
> others, which explains their need to clam up.
>   Sometimes, keeping the silence is used as a way to avoid one's
> own reality. When words are spoken, they reveal thoughts or
> fears of the thinker, which can be frightening. It can be used to
> mask fear, sullen anger, or it can be a spiteful refusal to co-
> operate.
>   This type of person can be maddeningly difficult to deal with
> because of the communication barrier they put up. *[Very like a
> teenage son!]* In most cases, this person will not be very willing
> to converse openly. When they speak, there might be prolonged
> periods of silence due to a lack of confidence in themselves and

their lives. This can result in a breakdown of communication, which leads to an unproductive interaction.

Those who portray this type of behaviour usually display such body language as staring, glaring, frowning, or folded arms in an uncomfortable fashion.

THE SUPER-AGREEABLE – A BIT LIKE A SPANIEL PUPPY!

The Super-agreeable is always reasonable, sincere, and supportive to your face, but doesn't always deliver as promised – with apologies to spaniel owners everywhere!

They want to be friends with everyone, love the attention. However, there's a darker side. They tend to lead you on with deceptive hints and references to problems that have been raised and will willingly agree to your plans of accomplishing the task at hand, only to let you down by not delivering them.

Back to Bramson for an astute description written some 13 years ago:

> Everyone needs to feel acceptance and to be liked by others. There is a balance point that integrates our needs to do a job well and to find a reasonable place in the pecking order with a reasonable concern for being liked.
>
> For this type of person, the burden is so far to one extreme that they feel an almost desperate need to be liked by everybody. Their method of gaining acceptance is to tell you things that are satisfying to hear. They also use humour as a way to ease their conversations with others.
>
> This type of difficult person presents a problem when they lead you to think that they are in agreement with your plans, only to let you down. Their strong need to give and receive friendship can conflict with the negative aspects of reality.
>
> Rather than directly losing friendships or approval, they will commit themselves to actions on which they cannot or will not follow through.

THE NEGATIVIST

The negative person is a corrosive influence on groups and can be very demotivating for the individual.

Here's another expert, the psychologist Rosner. Someone else you can quote from and sound like an expert!

> The Negativist is best described as a personality that not only disagrees with any cumulative suggestions in a group situation, but is also the first to criticise group progress. While their criticism could be interpreted as constructive, this disrupts progress in a work environment and could negatively impact interpersonal relationships within a working situation.
>
> Another common reference to the Negativist is the sceptic. Like the Negativist, these individuals like to tear apart and shoot holes in whatever is being said at the moment. They wear out their welcome over time as people catch on to their chronic negativity.
>
> Inside the character of a person who is considered to be negative is a person who is having difficulties dealing with a deep-seated inner conflict. This usually comes from a feeling that they don't have power over their own lives. The Negativist is unable to work through basic human disappointment. A Negativist believes that everyone can relate to and understand the well of disappointment they feel towards humanity and our own imperfection.
>
> While these people are so incredibly embittered about life and how it treats them, they are capable of having deep personal convictions at any task that is placed in front of them. However, if they are not in direct control of the project, it will fail because they believe that no one can handle or perform a task quite like they can.

THE KNOW-ALL

Know-alls have an overwhelming need to be recognised for their intellectual ability. They are bores, dull and very tedious!

Here are the thoughts of two eminent experts in the field of human behaviour. First Rafenstein:

> Know-alls can provoke feelings of anger, resentment, sometimes even violence in others.

So watch out! The second expert, Keyon, took a less alarming approach when writing in 1999:

> The Know-all could be suffering from lack of self-importance or may be unable to participate at the level in which he/she would like to contribute to the group's idea pool. Taking the time to listen to a Know-all's endless speeches could lead to loss of time in completing projects or assignments.

Know-alls are very complex people. They can be bullies. They appear so certain they are right, it seems pointless to argue. They can be very persuasive. They like to communicate like they are talking to a child. Very annoying!

The second Know-all type dominates conversations and likes being the centre of attention. The problem is, if they read a press cutting on a subject – they are an expert.

Some Know-alls are not above making up for any information or knowledge deficit by inventing a few facts.

Our friend Bramson wrote:

> Know-alls' problems stem from a need for others to think of them as being important and respected. Usually people who are confronted with a situation involving a Know-all are faced with a frustration. This usually leads to tension in work relationships.

THE INDECISIVE

Inside the Indecisive is a perfectionist trying to get out. They just can't seem to manage it. According to Bramson, this type of personality usually comes in two types. The first wants things done their way or no way; the second, at times, intentionally drags out discussions by injecting different viewpoints, frustrating everyone in the process.

> The indecisive person may be one who usually is not good at communicating their own thoughts, needs, and opinions to those around them. At best these people stall because they are unable to cope with stress at a high and low level.
>
> In order to deal with the stress they procrastinate, which brings down co-workers and other people around them. At best they stall by not considering alternative ways of getting a job done. So those on the receiving end of the indecision lose

enthusiasm and commitment to the project or person which eventually brings down the team.

Despite their success in evading the decision, the typical Indecisive gets stressed over a various amount of tension. This doesn't mean that they don't communicate a decision or feeling through indirect communications. In fact, they are masters in body language, low moans or grunts, or even eye contact.

If the Indecisive chooses to verbally make contact with other people it comes out in short phrases or sentences. Many times, these pieces of information get either ignored or shoved aside by co-workers who are already frustrated by the lack of communication they have received from that person.

They are also sensitive and might withhold information because they are worried about how it will be perceived by a group or person they are communicating it too. If the information is not sensitive they feel that their opinions don't matter and that someone else will deal with a conflict or problem that they are worried about.

...that's the end of the quick guide to the seven classic types. Now you're an expert. Make a coffee and let's put that new found knowledge to work!

Here are some more experts (more names to be flashy with!), who will give us a fast-track to dealing with difficult people.

First the diagnosis. What type are they? Brad McRae, author of *Negotiations and Influencing Skills: The Art of Creating and Claiming Value*, suggests there are four steps in the diagnosis.

- The first thing to do is to watch and take notice if you've seen this behaviour in three other situations with this person. The reason for this is that the first two times could be chance but by the third time it's probably a pattern.
- The second thing to do is to notice whether or not this person is dealing with a lot of stress. Stress may be causing this adverse behaviour and it may not be a regular occurrence.
- The third thing to do is to ask yourself whether *you've* been suffering from any exceptional stress. Stress on you may be causing you to see the world in a way that is contrary to what is actually going on.

- The fourth, have you had an adult-to-adult conversation with this person? There are times when the other person may, or may not, know that their behaviour is causing a problem for you and talking to them can clear up what turns out to be a simple misunderstanding.

McRae tells us: *'The reason people get into difficult situations with difficult people is because they allow themselves to become emotionally hooked. Often, the more we try to break free of these situations the more ensnared we become until some of us crack.'*

Why do we get hooked or sucked in to difficult people? Back to McRae: *'every person has a set of values or beliefs that guides their behaviour throughout life and especially in encounters with other people. Each set of values for each individual is different from another.'*

McRae listed fifteen of the most common core beliefs:

	Yup, that's me! ✔
I must be loved or accepted by everyone.	
I must be perfect in all I do.	
All the people with whom I work or live must be perfect.	
I can have little control over what happens to me.	
It is easier to avoid facing difficulties and responsibilities than to deal with them.	
Disagreement and conflict should be avoided at all costs.	
People, including me, do not change.	
Some people are always good; others always bad.	
The world should be perfect, and it is terrible and catastrophic when it is not.	
People are fragile and need to be protected from The Truth.	
Others exist to make me happy, and I cannot be happy unless others make me happy.	
Crises are invariably destructive, and no good can come from them.	

Somewhere there is the perfect job, the perfect solution, the perfect partner and so on, and all I need to do is search for them.	
I should not have problems. If I do, it indicates I am incompetent.	
There is one and only one way of seeing any situation – the true way.	

...time for a break. Have one of those quiet, reflective moments! You won't understand others if you don't understand yourself. Which of McRae's values do you share?

If you can, take a look at yourself and decide which core value is, or was, hooked in a particular difficult situation you've had to deal with. Now you will understand why you were upset. This new understanding leads to better control of yourself and your emotions.

According to McRae, if we are prepared to accept that the first step is to control ourselves, then we have a better chance to control others and the situations we find ourselves in.

Back to where we started, with the work of Robert Bramson. In his book, *Coping With Difficult People*, he lists tips for dealing with each of the seven types.

Here is his 'at a glance guide'!

The type	**The response**
The Hostile Sherman Tank	• Give them a little time to run down. • Don't worry about being polite; get in any way you can. • Get their attention, perhaps by calling them by name or sitting or standing deliberately. • Getting them to sit down is a good idea. • Maintain eye contact. • State your own opinions forcefully. • Don't argue with what the other person is saying or try to cut them down. • Be ready to be friendly.

The Hostile Sniper	• Smoke them out. Don't let social convention stop you. • Provide them with an alternative to a direct contest. • Don't focus on their point of view, be sure to involve everybody. • Do move fast to try to solve any problems that arise. • Prevent sniping by setting up regular problem-solving meetings. • If you are a witness to a situation with a Sniper, stay out of it, but insist that it stop in front of you.
The Hostile Exploder	• Give them time to run down on their own. • If they don't run down, cut into the tantrum with a neutral phrase such as 'Stop!' • Show them that you take them seriously. • If possible, take a breather with them to the side and in private.
The Complainer	• Listen attentively to their complaints even if you feel guilty or impatient. • Acknowledge what they are saying by paraphrasing their statements and checking out how you feel about it. • Don't agree or apologise for their allegation even if, at the moment, you accept it as true. • Avoid the accusation–defence–re-accusation ping-pong argument. • State and acknowledge facts without comment. • Try to move to a problem-solving mode by asking specific, information questions, assigning limited fact-finding tasks, or asking for the complaints in writing, but be serious and supportive about it. • If all else fails, ask the Complainer: *'How do you want this discussion to end?'*
The Silent Unresponsive	• Rather than trying to interpret what the silence means, get them to open up. • Ask open-ended questions. • Wait as calmly as you can for a response. • Use counselling questions to help move them along.

	• Do not fill in the silence with your conversation. • Plan enough time to allow you to wait with composure. • Get agreement on or state clearly how much time is set aside for your 'conversation'. • If you get no response, comment on what's happening. End your comment with an open-ended question. • Again, wait as long as you can, then comment on what's happening and wait again. Try to keep control of the interaction by dealing matter-of-factly with 'Can I go now?' and 'I don't know' responses. • When they finally open up: be attentive and watch your impulse to gush. Flow with tangential comments. They may lead you to something relevant and important. If they don't, state your own need to return to the original topic. • If they stay closed: avoid a polite ending, terminate the meeting yourself and set up another appointment. At length, inform them what you must do, since a discussion has not occurred.
The Super-agreeable	• You must work hard to surface the underlying facts and issues that prevent the Super-agreeable from taking action. • Let them know that you value them as people by telling them directly, asking or remarking about family, hobbies, apparel. Do this only if you mean it, at least a little! • Ask them to tell you those things that might interfere with your good relationship. • Ask them to talk about any aspect of your product, service, or self that is not as good as the best. • Be ready to compromise and negotiate if open conflict is in the wind. • Listen to their humour. There may be hidden messages in those quips or teasing remarks.

The Negativist	• Be alert to the potential, in yourself and in others in your group, for being dragged down into despair. • Make optimistic but realistic statements about past successes in solving similar problems. • Don't try to argue them out of their pessimism. • Do not offer solution-alternatives yourself until the problem has been thoroughly discussed and you know what you are dealing with. • When an alternative is being seriously considered, quickly raise the question yourself of negative events that might occur if the alternative were implemented. • At length, be ready to take action on your own. Announce your plans to do this without equivocation. • Beware of eliciting negativist responses from highly analytical people by asking them to act before they feel ready.
The Know-all	• Make sure you have done a thorough job of preparing yourself; carefully review all pertinent materials and check them for accuracy. • Listen carefully and paraphrase back the main points of the proposals, thus avoiding over-explanation. • Avoid dogmatic statements. • To disagree, be tentative, yet don't equivocate; use the questioning form to raise problems. • Ask extensional questions to assist in the re-examination of plans. • As a last resort, choose to subordinate yourself to avoid static and perhaps to build a relationship of equality in the future. Where the Know-all is not threatening or bullying: • State correct facts or alternative opinions as descriptively as possible and as your own perceptions of reality. • Provide a means for them to save face.

	• Be ready to fill a conversation gap yourself. • If possible, cope with them when they are alone.
The Indecisive	• Make it easy for the Indecisive to tell you about conflicts or reservations that prevent the decision. • Listen for indirect words, hesitations and omissions that may provide clues to problem areas. • When you have surfaced the issue, help them solve their problem with a decision. • At times, their reservations will be about you. If so, acknowledge any past problems and state relevant data non-defensively; propose a plan and ask for help. • If you are not part of the problem, concentrate on helping the Indecisive examine the facts. Use the facts to place alternative solutions in priority order. This makes it easier if they have to turn someone else down. • If real, emphasise the quality and service aspects of your proposal. • Give support after the decision seems to have been made. • If possible, keep the action steps in hands. • Watch for signs of abrupt anger or withdrawal from the conversation. If you see them, try to remove them from the decision situation.

Final thought. What could be more complex than human behaviour? The psycho-gurus spend their lives trying to make it easy for us, but in the workplace and at home it can get very complicated. The best advice is: deal with it and deal with it now.

The longer a difficult situation goes on and the longer you tolerate the behaviour of a difficult person, the harder it will be to sort it out. Unpick it and make it right. Yes, **D** stands for difficult, but it also stands for 'Do it now'.

OK, lecture over. What's your next letter?

To lead the people, walk behind them.

Lao Tzu

EFFECTIVE

effective adj.&n. *1 having a definite or desired effect 2 powerful in effect, impressive*

Well, that's what the dictionary tells us it means. I have another definition and as it's my A–Z, I think I'll use it:

> Effectiveness is putting words into deeds and getting results.

How many managers do you know who are members of the chattering classes? All talk and no delivery? Loads of things to say, opinions to express and comments to make? How effective are they? Zilcho, I bet! They gossip their way around the organisation until they get found out, or their budget explodes in someone's face.

There are all kinds of ineffective managers. Here's a short list of the ones to avoid:

- Committee managers – happily spend days in meetings, doing nothing and waging war on efficiency with a cup of tea and a ginger biscuit.
- Memo managers – they'll write to you until the last tree has been cut down from the last rainforest.
- Chatty managers – always willing to talk over a problem and never do anything effective about it.
- Flapper managers – possibly the most dangerous! Loads of action, running around, meeting after meeting and a diary full, not a moment to spare. All action no effect.
- Phone managers – always on the phone. Always engaged, line always busy. Never get out of the office to achieve anything.

Which one are you? None I hope. But, you may recognise a few colleagues!

What is the secret of effective people? Here are my top five things:

1 They always hire people who are better than they are. They step back
   and take the credit. To do otherwise means that at some stage you will
   have to step forward and take the blame!
2 They constantly audit themselves. They ask themselves: 'What am I
   going to achieve if I do this?'
3 When they get something wrong they are not afraid to look into the
   mirror and ask 'Why?' They want to know why they are not effective.
   What went wrong. Effective people have strange egos. In failure they
   have no ego and in success they have an ego they call 'pride in a job
   well done'.
4 Effective people review their effectiveness frequently. They want to
   know they are effective in everything they do. They ask: 'Am I being
   effective, right now?' They don't wait and they never kid themselves.
5 Effective people are results-led. They look for results in their own performance and in the performance of the people around them. They are
   often inspirational and seem to have the knack of managing their time to
   get results. They know how to prioritise.

Give yourself an effectiveness audit. Pick a day and make it your audit day.
Then ask yourself:

✍	Yes ✔	No ✔	Mmmm! ✔
Meetings:			
Was it effective?			
Was there a measurable outcome?			
Was I effective in the meeting? Did I have a worthwhile contribution to make?			
Was my being there making a difference?			
Communications:			
Have I cleared my inbox today?			
Is the stuff I have left really not do-able right now?			

	Yes ✓	No ✓	Mmmm! ✓
Would it be more effective to pass it on?			
Do I prioritise my response to mail? Have I set up appropriate files and auto-responses?			
Did I make all my call backs?			
Did I make time to network?			
Decisions:			
Have I made effective decisions, or put off making decisions?			
Do I measure the effectiveness of my decisions?			

✍ Finally: What are the words and actions I have taken today that have been effective for the organisation I work in and the people around me?
1
2
3
4
5
6
7
8
9
10

What kind of a day have you had? Er – pick another letter!

The quality of leadership, more than any other single factor,
determines the success or failure of an organisation.

Fred Fiedler & Martin Chemers

FACE TO FACE

face to face v. *1* *facing* *2* *confronting each other*

It is a bit of a pity that the dictionary definition of 'face to face' uses the word 'confronting'. It might give off the wrong message. This section is all about 'face-to-face management'. This is different. There is nothing confrontational about it. It does mean confronting issues and problems but it's not *confrontational*.

There is a growing tendency among managers to manage by remote control. Manage by memo, e-mail, voice mail. Managing face to face needs a different technique. It also takes planning, time, determination and courage.

Want to say 'well done'? Say it face to face. Somewhere in your organisation there is a back that needs patting – not someone aching to read a memo!

None of us like to deliver bad news, or confront poor performance or bad behaviour. In big organisations there is plenty of administrative undergrowth to hide in! It's easier to whizz off an e-mail.

Face-to-face managers command respect, are trusted and admired. So, how do you do it?

Let's start with a question:

Got bad news to deliver? How do you think the recipient wants to hear about it? Do they want to read it in a memo, or would they rather read it in the eyes of the responsible manager.

How many face-to-face contacts have you had in the last five days?

None? Some? How many?

Now answer the next question:

How many e-mails and memos have you sent out in the last five days?

Loads? Hundreds? How many?

Now ask yourself: how many of them could have been done face to face? Or, when push comes to shove, personally, over the telephone?

Personal contact produces trust. Almost everything else creates an opportunity for mistrust and misinterpretation.

Here are ten steps to becoming a face-to-face manager.

1 Got information you want the organisation to hear? Do it face to face. Organise a communications day. Brief staff and colleagues in groups. In small organisations, or departments, it won't take long. In big organisations it could take all day. So, start early in the morning and carry on for as long as it takes. Brief groups on the hour, every hour. Use the same materials, the same colleagues to do it with and deliver your message to everyone, face to face. That way you will kill gossip and speculation and be sure your message gets across – face to face. It is hard work and not something you might want to do every day – but it works!

2 If you work in a large organisation, vary your way in, in the morning. Don't use the same door. Try going in around the back, through another department, use a different lift or stairway. On the way, say good morning to five people. Introduce yourself and ask them what they do. Ask 'How are things?' They will be amazed and you might be surprised at what they tell you! One thing you can rely on is this: the five people you meet will tell five of their colleagues all about it!

3 Ring-fence some time in your diary to go walkabout. Get out from behind your desk and get into the organisation and talk to people, face to face. If the place where you work uses shift work, make some time to visit late at night or early in the morning. American management guru, Tom Peters, preached 'management by walking about'. He's right. The only piece of kit you need, to be a modern, face-to-face manager, is a decent pair of shoes!

4 Give yourself a target. Find five people a week who deserve a 'well done' or a pat on the back and do it personally. Face to face.

5 Got bad news or a criticism to make? Do it face to face. Not in your office. Go to the person or department concerned, find a quiet place and say what you want to say face to face: *'This is difficult for us all, but I wanted to be honest with you. I'm not happy with (this or that). I wanted to tell you personally and give you the chance to let me hear your side of the story…'*

6 Have an open door policy – and mean it. Prop your door open with something conspicuous. A china dog, or a brass weight. Make it clear to people: when the door is open, you welcome visitors. When the door is shut, they should respect your privacy. Don't expect staff to make an

appointment to see you – unless they want to. If you are there, and free, you'll talk, answer questions and deal with things face to face.

7   Can't do it all face to face and have to use the telephone? That's OK, but have a *face to face* phone policy. Accept all your own calls. Don't hide behind an assistant. If you are there and the phone rings – pick it up and deal *face to face*!

8   Really, really stuck for a face to face? Try texting! Most staff and colleagues have mobile phones. Software for what is known as broadcast-texting is a cheap download from the Internet. You can text up to a thousand mobile phones simultaneously. It's not as good as face to face, but it is instant and can be used to kill gossip or pass on urgent news.

9   Don't think newsletters replace the face to face. In small organisations they are superfluous and in large organisations they are almost entirely useless. Think about it: in a large organisation you will have people who read and enjoy *The Times* as their source of daily news. Others will read the *Guardian* and a lot will want *The Mirror* or *Sun*. And everything in between, including the *Financial Times* and the *Daily Star*! Each of those newspapers has a different style, intellectual framework and approach. They may be newspapers, but they are really only products reaching a target market. So, how can newsletters reach out, appeal to and be read by such a diverse audience? Answer: they can't. They end up in the bin!

10   Set yourself a target of making at least one new face-to-face contact every day!

OK, next letter please Carol!

Skill in the art of communication is crucial to a leader's success. They can accomplish nothing unless they can communicate effectively.

Norman Allen

G

GLORY

glory n.&v. *1 high renown, fame, honour 2 adoring 3 praise the bliss and splendour of heaven*

 **Hazard Warning**

As a manager, if you are any good at what you do, well balanced, can exercise sound judgement and are confident, you won't look for 'glory'.

 Tip

Glory is something to give away. Give the glory of success to the people you work with, the team who work for you, the organisation that backs you. There's nothing more to be said.

Think about it. Praise, acclamation, applause, commendation, kudos, acclaim – you don't need it. You know how good you are and what a great job you are doing. Give the glory to the others.

Next letter, please...

There are no office hours for leaders.

Cardinal J Gibbons

H

HAPPY

happy adj. *1 feeling of showing pleasure or contentment 2 fortunate, characterised by happiness*

Is everybody happy? They are? Great! How do you know? Happy in the sense of motivated, not in the sense of off your face! Happy staff do a better job. Trite? Overused? Hackneyed? Yes, of course. But like all of these old wives' tales and clichéd sayings, they contain huge amounts of truth. Good old solid, common-sense truth.

How do you know if people are happy? Managers' perceptions of what is going on, how people are feeling, often lag behind the truth. Good managers are right on top of the job, get out and about in their organisations and develop a feeling for gauging levels of morale and motivation. Nevertheless, they often miss the signs. Here's why.

- For whatever reason, some people hide their feelings and are very good at disguising how they really feel.
- Macho management styles discourage openness and encourage people to hide their feelings.
- Office politics and peer pressure can encourage a cover-up.
- Office bullying can create a fear of reprisals if people speak out.
- The culture of the organisation can create an environment where 'it just isn't done'.
- People are too willing to please.
- People don't want to look disruptive.
- People don't understand the real issues.
- There is no time.
- Poor communications and a feeling of 'no one is listening, anyway'.

Based on the work of Patrick Forsyth in *How to Motivate People* (2000), Kogan Page, London.

Some bright management guru, with a brain the size of Milton Keynes (I can't remember exactly which one it was), said 'management is measurement and everything is measurable'.

So, can you measure organisational happiness? You sure can. But, you have to have the systems in place. Here is a selection of ideas:

- Ask people: 'Are you happy?' Simple enough. Managers should regularly debrief their staff.
- Tell managers they are responsible for making sure staff are happy and motivated. Put it in the job description.
- If you pay peanuts you get monkeys – grumpy monkeys. May sure pay structures contribute to motivation.

 Tip

Need to communicate something with staff urgently? Try sending a text message. Invite staff who have mobile phones (and who doesn't these days?) to put their numbers on a central database, so that they can be kept bang up to date with the latest organisation news. Software to do this is a low cost investment. Not all staff have mobile telephones? Don't worry, rely on the ones that do to spread the message to the ones that don't.

- Be open with people, communicate with them, regularly – face to face, targeted newsletters, noticeboards, tapes and text messages – and avoid the corrosive effects of gossip.
- Social events – make sure they are appropriate. Golf days can be a turn-off for the non-golfers. Avoid macho interests. A visit to a lap-dancing club is a no-no for mixed sex groups. Try and find things to do that will involve staff's partners who do not work for the company – family days and so on.
- Use annual appraisal interviews to ask questions about workplace happiness and motivation.
- Have effective policies on absenteeism and discipline.
- Motivation schemes such as employee of the month – monitor them and make them work for you by focusing attention on the good things that people do.

Happy people don't go sick so often as the miserable ones!

Poor morale can lead to endemic lead-swinging. Departments become unmanageable because everyone is using sickness as a way of forgetting their problems at the office.

Here's a neat solution – measure absences. This is how it's done:

- days off sick either side of a weekend – score 10 points
- days off sick either side of a bank holiday – score 12 points
- single days off sick during the week – score 8 points
- linked mid-week days off sick – score 2 points a day
- days off for long-term sickness – score 1 point per week.

Use a period of not less than a month and not more than a quarter. This weighted method of scoring highlights the obvious skivers and does not penalise those who are genuinely ill.

Now add up the scores for each department and publish the results on the intranet, e-mail or noticeboard. Be sure everyone sees the results.

Expect the following to happen:

- Demonstrating that the issue has management attention will impact the lead-swingers and reduce sickness absences immediately.
- Departments with a high score will probably be the poor performers and will be impacting on other departments. Expect peer pressure to leverage down unacceptable and unwarranted absence levels.

Want to know how people feel? Ask them to fill out a questionnaire like this. No names, no pack-drill...

My work here is made more difficult by .... and would be made easier if .... I would/ would not recommend a friend to work here because .... I am always set/never set realistic targets and I always/never have a meaningful input and I always/never get feedback on my performance. If the organisation were an animal, it would be a .... and if it were a piece of furniture, it would be a ....

...go on, I dare you!

THINGS ARE CHANGING – IS EVERYBODY HAPPY?

Morale at the time of organisational change is at its most brittle. Tricky time. The idea is to keep everyone focused on the big picture and keep them motivated along the way. For example, changing the NHS has been likened to turning a supertanker – takes time and can't be done on a sixpence.

At the first sign of change morale usually increases, but as time goes by it sinks, until the effect of improvements can be seen by everyone. This 'trough' effect is typical.

The idea is to keep the trough as shallow and narrow as possible. This is achieved by having a number of high profile, low cost quick fixes that can be phased in along the way, whilst the big changes take time to come into effect.

When people can see things changing, they seldom worry about evaluating the changes in terms of money. The impact on their working day is the most important thing to them.

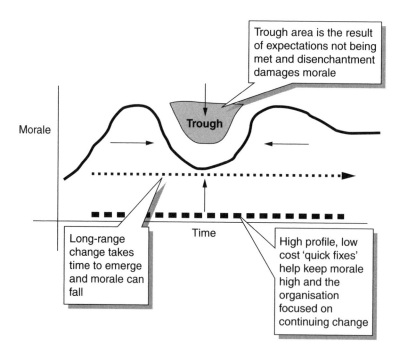

Organisations with no meaningful incentives of their own end up being managed by airline bonus miles programmes.

INSPIRATION

inspiration n. *1* *a supposed creative force or influence* *2* *sudden brilliant, creative or timely idea*

A great man once said: 'Where there is perspiration, there is inspiration.' Like the golfer who was accused by his playing partner of being 'lucky'. He replied: 'The more I play, the luckier I get!'

The more you do, the better you get.

Well, that's probably true. But there is a contradiction here. Doing a lot of the same means it is easy to get into a rut. Do the same thing every day, do the same job and a strange thing happens. Funnily enough, it's another 'I' word:

Invisible

The organisation and the people you work with become invisible. In the same way that you don't see the stain on the kitchen floor and the tiny piece of wallpaper peeling off the wall in the hallway, the things we see every day we no longer notice.

So, how do you dig your way out of a rut? Where do you go to find inspiration? Well, not necessarily to an international motivational guru, or to the top of a Nepalese mountain for a session with your spiritual advisor. Mind you, if it works for you – good luck!

You might find some inspiration closer to home. The people you work with, for instance. Got a problem? Short on inspiration? Can't find the answer? You could always try the staff! Sit down with them, explain the problem and ask them what they think the answer might be.

Get a list of solutions, and then here's a neat trick: accept the solution on the basis that whoever came up with the idea has the responsibility for implementing it. This has the effect of limiting excesses in solutions and in the longer run, is very empowering for staff.

Need some more inspiration? Let's put some building blocks in place. Make a list.

✍ What inspires you?

1

2

3

4

5

6

7

✍ When do you feel inspired?

1

2

3

4

5

6

7

✍ Who inspires you?

1

2

3

4

5

6

7

✍ Why were you inspired?

1

2

3

4

5

6

7

Having trouble with the answers? Have an inspired guess! Play around with ideas. The more you exercise your mind, the more inspired you will be.

You are aiming to discover what are the circumstances, who are the people and where are the places that spark inspiration.

What are the best ideas you've ever come up with? Where were you and who were you with when the light-bulb came on? Can you recreate the circumstances?

Relying on tried and tested solutions is tempting, but can you move on? Can you try another approach?

 Exercise

Think about the jobs, the tasks, the processes that are stuck in a rut.

Pick one and look for an inspired solution. Brainstorm, look for ideas 'outside the box'. Talk to colleagues. Talk to people in different industries that might be facing similar problems. What do they do? Replicate the circumstances when the light-bulb came on and you were inspired and apply them to this issue.

Technology has met its promise of reducing our workload.
It does this, primarily, by preventing us from doing any work at all!

J

JUDGEMENT

judgement n. *1 the critical faculty, discernment 2 good sense*

The opposite to judgement, in my view, is prejudice. Prejudice is corrosive and a threat to fair and objective judgement. To be prejudiced by the way someone looks, dresses, speaks, behaves, is a lack of judgement. Nice people are not always like us.

Here's a phrase worth cutting out and sticking on a wall:

> If we were born where they were born
> and taught what they had been taught,
> we would be like them.

This is not only about racial, religious or sexual prejudice. This is a lot about managers who make prejudiced decisions about people, staff and events.

Staff, suppliers and people who use your services need a fair hearing and for you to exercise sound judgement. How to do it? Easy; stick to the facts and if you don't know the facts, don't make a judgement until you do. Avoid the subjective and try to be objective.

Do you think you'd pass the Judgement test? Here it is, give it a try!

Think about the last time you made a really important 'people decision'. I can't bear the phrase 'human resources' and I don't like 'personnel', so if it's OK with you, I'll stick with 'people'!

If you don't do 'people decisions' pick another event where you had a tough call to make.

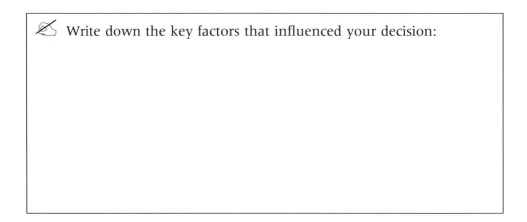

Did you have all the facts? All the information?

Now go and find a mirror. Look at yourself and say:

> 'My decision was wholly objective and the best one I could have made in the circumstances. I did not allow my prejudices to influence me.'

Feel comfortable with that? Good, you passed the test. Be sure and ask yourself that question each time you have a big call to make.
    Ready for a **K**?

Organisations are generally slow to adopt new ways of business, especially if it means a reduction in their beloved paper!

KNOWLEDGE

knowledge n. *1 awareness or familiarity gained by experience 2 the sum of what is known 3 certain understanding*

I'm not much of a one for management fads. You know, the sort of thing that management gurus come up with from time to time. Ideas that are supposed to revolutionise our thinking, change what we do, streamline our lives and turn our pretty brain-boxes inside out. We've had:

- The Vision Thing
- The Mission Thing
- Direction Setting
- Flat Organisation Theory
- Decoding Corporate Culture
- Open Environments
- Empowerment
- Customer Focus
- The Value Revolution
- Total Quality Management
- Re-engineering.

 Tip

For the really irreverent amongst you there is a great book debunking most of this stuff. It is called *Fad Surfing in the Boardroom* by Eileen Shapiro, published by Capstone.* Well worth a read!

Some of it is just new metaphors for well-established management practice and some of it, frankly, I find *aloadarubbish*!

That said, I think there is one new management 'invention' that is well worth a look.

---

* Shapiro EC (1996) *Fad Surfing in the Boardroom: reclaiming the courage to manage in the age of instant answers.* Capstone, Oxford.

KNOWLEDGE MANAGEMENT

There are lots of definitions. Here's mine:

> Collecting and making accessible all of the information the organisation has, to help people do a better job for the customer.

Think of it another way. Knowledge management can:

- gather information on best practice and share it across the organisation
- identify barriers to peak performance
- support 'communities' of workers
- develop self-help information strategies
- help develop and achieve objectives.

Ask yourself and your colleagues: how do you share information?

In the health service, important records, patients' notes and test results are, for the most part, hand-written and stored in envelopes. The result is that the information is difficult to share and very prone to going astray. The consequence is delays, inconvenience and who knows, perhaps even lives lost.

In the commercial world, modern companies keep their information in data-warehouses on the Internet or intranets. This means you can go into a store at one end of the country and they will be able to confirm your purchase in a store at the other end and give you a refund.

Call up a computer software helpline and the technician will have access to an Internet knowledge base, to figure out a solution to your problem. Supermarkets have loyalty cards from which they can tell what you buy and when you buy it. That way they can be sure to stock lines that are selling well and introduce you to new products. Buy a holiday from the Internet and you will be offered car hire, reading material about your destination and even a loan to finance it.

In the real world companies are using information to provide you with better and faster services and to develop a relationship with you. Indeed there is another management fad–speak–guru–whizzo–idea called *relationship marketing*. But that is a story for another time! Mind you, it is a good story!

There are three elements to getting knowledge management sorted:

- understanding
- channels
- collaboration.

Let's have a look at them in turn.

UNDERSTANDING

The question is: do your staff and colleagues know how best to share learning and experiences with their colleagues? Don't take it for granted that they do. In a survey of staff working in a global finance company (who are supposed to be good at this sort of thing), only 27% said they knew how best to share information.

So, what's it like over at your place? Don't know? Well, ask the question, do a survey.

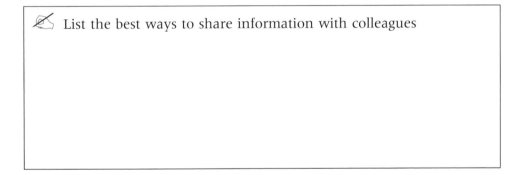

List the best ways to share information with colleagues

CHANNELS

Knowledge management is really a product of the intranet age. However, research shows that levels of awareness amongst staff can be low and they often do not understand the extent of the facilities on offer. Acceptance is low. From the same survey of global finance whizz-kids, only one-third said they regularly posted information on their intranet, to share knowledge.

If the place you work in doesn't have an intranet there are two things you can do. You can get a friendly anorak to pop in and create one for you. Most computers running Windows (and whose doesn't?) have a facility called Neighbourhood Network. You can link computers together and share files and systems. Search the help files under 'networking' and read all about it.

The second thing you can do is arrange knowledge sharing sessions. Set aside 15 minutes a week to network information with colleagues. If you have regular meetings, timetable a slot at the end for knowledge sharing. It's not ideal, but anything is better than nothing.

COLLABORATION

Once you have the basics in place you need to measure and get a feel for what is working and what isn't. Back to the survey of the finance whizz-kids. Only 23% of them found it was easy to share best practice. In this case the company dug into what was happening and presented examples of best practice in knowledge sharing to a sceptical and confused staff. Where they demonstrated positive benefits the staff soon picked up the idea and got on the knowledge wagon.

 Can you list some examples of how sharing knowledge has improved service delivery where you work?

The American business and IT firm, AMS, employs 8750 employees in 51 offices around the world. They decided they needed to act on the knowledge management (KM) front and asked themselves seven very sensible questions.

- Where does KM fit into the organisation's existing strategy?
- Is the organisation ready for it?
- What is its strategic role?
- Who are the key stakeholders?
- Will the organisation's culture support it?
- How will it be measured?
- Will it bring value to the customers?

 These are good questions to ask. How would you adapt them to make them relevant to where you work?

-
-
-
-
-
-
-

The fundamentals of getting KM up and running involve focusing on the people, the processes in place, what information you already have, and the sharing methods.

Knowledge is power and getting people to share it means, for some, a loss of power and status. Bear that in mind.

 Tip

Tempted and want to know more? Here's a great starter book – *Knowledge Management and Business Model Innovation*.* It has a great slug on how traditional bricks-and-mortar outfits turned into clicks-and-mortar enterprises.

Sharing information and knowledge might be as simple as insisting, every time someone attends a conference and seminar, that when they come back to the ranch they do a short presentation and pass on the key learning facts they picked up. On the other hand it may be as complex as databases for accessing customer files (or in the case of the NHS, patient files).

Knowledge management is an organisational asset that prevents waste, stops folk reinventing the wheel and speeds up response. All organisations and departments have information. It is priceless and worth digging for. Don't get swept away with technology, you can do KM with or without it. And, in any case, the technology isn't that difficult.

Next letter please...

---

* Malhotra Y (ed.) (2001) *Knowledge Management and Business Model Innovation*. Ideal Group Publishing, London.

Managing means leading, making things happen through people: for me that is relevant to all levels of management, not just the top management.

Sir Peter Parker

L

LEADERSHIP

leader n. *1 a person or thing that leads; a person followed by others **2** the principal player*

Say the word 'Mandela' and what word do you think of? How about Churchill, Nelson or Wellington? Then again, there is Shearer, Beckham, Redgrave, Lara, Madonna, Mountbatten, Reith, Walesa, Theresa, Wilson, Hillary, Disraeli, Gladstone, Botham, Altman. And, let's not forget Amin, Hussein and Hitler!

I guess the word we think of has to be 'leader'.

Those whom we recognise as 'leaders' come in all shapes and sizes. They come in all guises and from all backgrounds and walks of life. They have wonderful motives and sinister motives. They are everywhere. Leaders in fashion, pop, business, politics and sport. How about where you work? How many leaders are there?

Is your boss or manager a leader? Probably not! In most work environments bosses become the boss because they are next in line. In sales companies the head honcho is invariably a salesperson. In accounting firms the boss is usually an accountant. Engineers usually run engineering businesses. Because they are the boss or the manager does not make them great leaders.

In big organisations it is not unusual to find people with real qualities of leadership who are quite junior, or way down the food chain.

So what is the difference between a manager and a leader?

MANAGERS AND LEADERS – SPOT THE DIFFERENCE

A manager is a *copy*, who *administers* and *maintains*. Managers will *focus on structures* and *rely on control*. Generally, they will have a *short-range view* and ask questions like *How?* and *When?*

Managers have an *eye on the bottom line* and *accept the status quo*. Nevertheless, they are the *classic good soldier* who *does things right*.

On the other hand...

A leader is an *original*, who *innovates* and *develops*. Leaders will *focus on people* and *inspire trust*. Generally, they will have a *long-range perspective* and ask questions like *What?* and *Why?* Leaders have an *eye on the horizon* and *challenge the status quo*. They are *their own person* who *does the right thing*.

Let's look at those words another way. Here is a direct comparison. Use the table to rate yourself (or your manager!). Be honest.

Leader	Yup ✔	Manager	Yup ✔
Original		Copy	
Innovates		Administrates	
Develops		Maintains	
Focuses on people		Focuses on structure	
Inspires trust		Relies on control	
Long-range perspective		Short-range view	
Asks What? and Why?		Asks How? and When?	
Eye on the horizon		Eye on the bottom line	
Challenges the status quo		Accepts the status quo	
Is their own person		Classic good soldier	
Does the right thing		Does things right	
Total ticks		Total ticks	

There are 11 qualities. What's the score? Any less than nine and I'd say you're looking at a follower. What do you think?

I say there are nine rules that are all about being a leader.

1 BE VISIBLE

Leaders don't hide. You can lead from the front, you can lead from the high ground, but you cannot lead from behind closed doors.

Top people in the organisation must demonstrate they have a genuine interest in it. Being visible helps demonstrate that interest. Being invisible does not. Being visible is about being in touch with the organisation, understanding its thinking and capturing its mood.

There are limitless ways of getting a message into an organisation: e-mail, texting, memos, newsletters and all the rest. The best way to convince someone of your sincerity and commitment is face to face. Let them read it in your eyes. Employees' confidence that the top people know what they are doing comes best from face to face encounters.

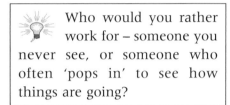 Who would you rather work for – someone you never see, or someone who often 'pops in' to see how things are going?

I am a passionate believer in the theory of 'management by walking about'. The phrase comes from a great book, by American management guru Tom Peters, called *In Pursuit of Excellence*. I have had the good fortune to meet Tom and I asked him, as the book had been published many years ago, whether it was still valid. He agreed that much had moved on and the world of 'quality re-engineering' had changed. However, he said one thing hadn't changed, the importance of management by walking about. He's dead right.

People often say to me something to the effect that they work in a big organisation and it's tough to do it. My answer is always the same. Being visible is not an optional extra, it is as much part of management and leadership as understanding the balance sheet and being able to write a decent report.

Try this:

- Get to work 11 minutes early each morning for a week. Use the time to follow a different route to your office each morning and make a point of introducing yourself to five members of staff. By the end of the week you will have met 25 people, who in turn will have each told five more people that they've met you. Those five will tell another five and before you know it, half the western world will know what a decent, caring, interested person you are.

• Got an important message to get over to the staff? Try having a communications day. Arrange for you and the manager most involved in the issue to hold briefing sessions for every member of staff. Plan a 20 minute session and have them in a central point. Hold them every hour on the hour, from 6 am through to 11 pm. Yes, it will be a long day. But if the issues are important enough, you will go home happy in the knowledge that everyone has had the message, from the same people and in the same way. There will be no room for gossip and no room for misunderstanding. Montgomery used to do it, standing on a tank. If it was good enough for him, it's good enough for the rest of us!

> There was once a great debate about who was the best leader, Gladstone or Disraeli. It fell to Queen Victoria's granddaughter, Princess Marie Louise, to provide the answer. She dined one evening with Gladstone and the next with Disraeli.
>
> She said, 'When I left the table having dined with Mr Gladstone I thought he was the cleverest man in England. But when I dined with Mr Disraeli, I thought I was the cleverest woman in England'.

2 MEASURE WHAT IS DONE

Measuring? What has that got to do with leadership? Good question. The answer is: this is about measuring what is done against a handful of fundamental criteria – I call that the 'zero-base' of the organisation. A zero-base can be expressed as the mission for the organisation. A commitment to a set of shared values that the whole organisation can sign up to. Fundamental truths. The foundation stone for what is done, every day, a signpost for the future and a yardstick against which to measure progress. Leaders have their yardstick, their foundation beliefs and they share them with everyone.

Each decision is tested by the question 'does what we are doing match up to the organisation's values?' This is a constant process and comes second nature to leaders.

3 Set an example

Is this too obvious? Well, perhaps not. Think about this: there was, once, a big media furore over whether or not Master Leo Blair had had his MMR jab. His Dad, the nation's leader, said he wasn't going to discuss the medical history of his kids in public. All very reasonable.

But! A large slice of the great British public took the view that they had every right to know. They said: 'If he wants us to jab our kids, we have every right to know if he's jabbed his own.' A mischievous press and a medical profession that seemed unable to get its act together conspired to make a difficult situation obscure. Was it safe to jab our youngsters with a cocktail of immunisation jollop, or would it be better to do it a bit at a time?

Here's the question: as a leader, should the boss have led by example and told us what he had done?

Not easy being a leader, is it? What would you have done? Do as I tell you, or do as I do?

One thing is true: successful organisations achieve more from their staff by way of commitment than average outfits do and that invariably comes from following the example of the people at the top. The more a leader does, the more everyone else will do. 'Nuff said?

4 Get the organisation right

Leaders get the organisation right and then look after the staff as a result of having a successful organisation. A well-organised, successful organisation is a good place to work. No one likes to work in a mess, or in an atmosphere of indecision. The success of any organisation is dependent on the skills and talents of the people who work in the organisation. It is usually the case that the majority of an organisation's resources is spent on staffing costs. Staff are the most valuable asset you have.

A successful organisation is a secure organisation, able to devote time and money to its workforce.

A well-led, successful organisation can afford to look after the people who have contributed to its success. An organisation struggling for survival cannot.

> Leaders hire people who are better than they are, step back and take the credit. The others hire people who are worse than they are and one day will have to step forward to take the blame.

Getting the organisation 'right' is sometimes a tough nut to crack. It might mean there are too many people, poorly trained people or people who are not good enough. Leaders don't step back from tough decisions. They know the foundations have to be right.

5 BE INNOVATIVE

Leaders have a continuous interest in innovation and the process of change. Time and new ideas wait for no one. It is a commonly identifiable habit of leaders that they are constantly searching for new and better ways.

Innovation is the mark of a leader. They know introducing change can be a nightmare, but they don't shrink from doing it. Leaders have an eye on the horizon and are prepared for the fact that change is the first step to success.

6 BE CLEAR ABOUT WHAT YOU WANT

Leaders have a clear vision, which they believe in passionately and share with everyone around them. Enthusiasm is infectious and a great motivator. Enthusiasm will thrive where people have the same vision and a common commitment to achieve.

What do you 'want'? What is your vision? Try filling in the blanks:
   My vision is .... (by/how) .... to .... (what you want to do) .... that .... (your unique objective) .... by .... (how you intend to achieve it) ....

All the really good leaders I have ever met have strong imaginations. They work on the basis 'if they can imagine it, it will happen'.

Bill Gates, the boss of Microsoft, says 'we are only limited by the imaginations of the people who work here'. But he wasn't the first business leader to recognise the importance of imagination; years earlier Walt Disney said 'our success is our imagination'.

Imagination is such a strong, repeating theme in the analysis of leadership that I have coined the word Imaginizor! You won't find it in the dictionary (yet!), but if you did, this is how it would be defined...

> Imaginizor/imæjeniǯœr/n.
> **1** One who can form mental images. **2** Being unrestricted by format.
> **3** Free thinking within the bounds of imagination. **4** Belief in the concept
> 'if you can imagine it, it will happen'.

Do you recognise yourself?

7 CREATE A CULTURE

Leaders are more interested in building a corporate culture than building a
corporate organisation. A team of bright people with a positive attitude will
give you an answer to a problem faster than a committee resigned to a world
full of problems. Leaders constantly re-examine the organisation to see
which bits have grown since it was last reviewed. A team works together for
a common goal; a committee can be full of representatives, each with a quite
separate agenda from the main one.

8 ACTIVE LEADERS ARE INSPIRATIONAL

Leaders are proactive, rather than reactive. Leaders are active and in-touch
and are therefore able to avoid most corporate surprises.

9 LEADERS ARE WINNERS

Leaders inspire organisations to succeed. They develop a culture of
achievement and enthusiasm for better performance which leads to the
excitement of winning – and that makes it all worthwhile!

I KNOW IT'S NOT EASY

I have run organisations in the private sector, been the leader of a council
and chaired an NHS Trust. In between I've run and done all sorts. Thus you
will see I am a professional has-been! However, most of those roles have had
an element of leadership. Now, having no 'proper job', I am able to look

back on what I've done (and not done) with a certain amount of pragmatism. Pragmatism being code for embarrassing honesty.

Of all the stuff I've done, I found the most difficult to get to grips with was
chairing an NHS Trust. Hospitals are complex organisations, convoluted,
intricate and perplexing. They are a minefield of special interest, tribalism
and the downright bloody-minded. They are also places of great inspiration,
motivation and miracles by the minute.

I found the competing priorities unfathomable and the whole thing a
Rubik's cube. I came from a world that was fast to respond, that had a more
cohesive view of itself and was not dammed by outside interference. We
just got-on-and-did-stuff. I came very close to throwing in the towel. I was
frustrated, angry and going nowhere.

Then I met a wise man!

He said to me: 'Is it any wonder you're making no progress? You are new,
a novelty and a threat. They haven't got a clue who you are, what you want
to do and how you think. Write down a set of beliefs, share them with
everyone and press on. They may not all agree, but at least they will know
what they are disagreeing with.'

In other words: leaders have vision and they share it with the people
around them. Good advice! So, I sat down and wrote a set of beliefs. Here
they are:

1 Place patients, residents and carers in the role of customers whose business is valuable – they, after all, have paid for the service we give. We
   must recognise that we are the hired help and the key to our growth is
   through the satisfaction of those we serve.
2 Plan for the future but be flexible enough to take advantage of the
   opportunities that present themselves as time passes.
3 Challenge every value, method and practice every day, in a never-ending
   search for something better.
4 Regard staff as an asset: pay them on their performance; seek to train,
   motivate and empower them to achieve more; make it clear that they are
   valued as part of a team and that they should look for what they can do
   for the organisation before they look for what the organisation can do for
   them. The organisation's success is their success – if the organisation fails,
   everyone will fail.
5 Create an image that is efficient, warm, trustworthy and responsive in an
   environment that is safe and clean.
6 Always have an idea on the horizon, and look for opportunities and
   ideas.

You may say – and I would agree – that this is not rocket science. However, for an NHS that was on the point of the Thatcher reforms of the late eighties and early nineties, these beliefs were a declaration of war!

Patients were never thought of as customers. Even today, there is a large group of NHS staff who have difficulty with the concept. The very idea that someone might make a virtue out of changing their mind was incomprehensible. Linking staff remuneration to performance is still a notion that the public sector has problems with.

So, what happened? Well, not a lot really! Some of the staff thought I was the devil in a pinstriped suit and my statement of beliefs confirmed it. Others thought I was a breath of fresh air and did everything they could to get behind my ideas and push. I was blessed with a really bright board and senior management team. They saw value in me setting out my stall, so everyone knew the framework they were working in.

It cleared the air, set the lines in the sand and everyone got on with the job.

What about you? Do you have a personal set of beliefs? Leaders have a vision and they share it. Share yours. Make a start right here. Use the matrix to get you thinking. Use it only as a start. These are your beliefs, not mine. Just use the grid to get going:

Beliefs	What do you say?
Role of the 'customer'	
Flexibility of approach	
Attitude to established values	
Staff	
Image	
The future	

Apart from the known and the unknown, what else is there?

Harold Pinter

MISTAKES

mistake n.&v. *1 an incorrect idea or opinion; a thing incorrectly done or thought 2 an error of judgement*

Let's get this right. A mistake is an error, an incorrect idea, or something incorrectly done. It is not a capital offence, a heinous crime or an occasion for a public flogging.

In the best of well-run organisations, from time to time, things will go wrong. Provided it doesn't happen too often, it is not a sin. What is a sin is getting something wrong, not doing something about it, not fixing it, or worst of all, not knowing something has gone wrong.

So, you've made a mistake. What should you do? Own up – that's what you should do. However, it is not as easy as that, is it? If you do own up are you likely to get a public roasting, be made to look a fool, or worse, get the sack?

The trick is to create a working environment where making a mistake is something that is not necessarily encouraged but is not universally condemned, either. British Airways, who know a thing or two about safety and getting the best out of their staff, have a great idea.

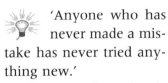 'Anyone who has never made a mistake has never tried anything new.'
Albert Einstein

They have a Senior Captain, who acts like the Pope. He hears the confessions of other pilots who might have made a mistake. Pressing the wrong button, skipping a procedure or forgetting something. Not in themselves capital offences, but if recorded and analysed, they could create reasons for redesigning a flight deck, changing the ergonomics or modifying rostering or working patterns. The 'Pope' hears the 'confession' in confidence and feeds the information into the risk management system, so that everyone can learn, develop and move on. Great idea. The NHS, well known for its mistakes, is working on a similar system for doctors and nurses. Well overdue, some would say.

In a world full of lawyers, litigation and a compensation culture, a blame-free working environment is not the easiest thing in the world to achieve. But, unless you can achieve it, you will never know how good your organisation could be and how bad it really is.

If you can create an environment where someone who has made a mistake can do these two things – you've cracked it! If you work somewhere that can't do this – think about working someplace else. Or, are you the manager and the problem?

	That's what we do! ✔
1 Tell your manager. Never try to hide an error. It is only when the organisation knows what has happened that they can fix it.	
2 Make sure there is a system to make recommendations on how to remedy the mistake. The experts at fixing problems are not the management gurus and grey suits, but the people who made the mistake in the first place. They know exactly what needs to be done to make sure it doesn't happen again.	

👍 Tips

Made a real howler? Try this.

Be upfront. Notify your boss immediately. Say how bad you feel. By saying sorry and letting them know you're aware of the seriousness of what you've done, they will know that you have learnt and will be more careful next time.

Don't hope it will go away by itself. The people where you work will support you if you are honest. Ask for help and enlist the help of whoever you need to solve the problem. Don't blame someone else. When the truth comes out you'll have to take the rap anyway, but you'll also look less trustworthy if you try and dump on a colleague.

Dealing with the consequences of a mistake? Talking to a 'customer' (whatever that means to you)? Think about it from the other side of the desk.

Try the PLUSH system, the only luxury way to handle organisational mistakes:

- **Pause**: Stop what you're doing and give the individual with the complaint your full attention.
- **Listen**: Let the individual know you are listening, either by asking questions or making notes. Face to face – plenty of head nodding. On the phone, ask questions.
- **Understand**: Use questions to get the facts and repeat them back – show you understand the issues. Don't jump to conclusions.
- **Solve**: Let the person know what you are suggesting to solve the problem, what steps you propose to take and what the time scales are – and acknowledge the mistake.
- **Hercules**: Make Herculean attempts to keep to deadlines. If you are unable to get back with a solution or suggestions, or you find something you said you'd do is undoable, be sure to call or write and say so and agree another deadline.

Next letter? How many have you done?

Leadership is one of those elusive qualities, an area where there is no absolute, no guaranteed model.

Sir Peter Parker

N

NETWORK

network n.&v. *1 an arrangement of intersecting horizontal and vertical lines 2 a group of people who exchange information, contacts and experiences for social and professional purposes*

Well, you know what they say: 'When all else fails, quote your mother.' So, here goes:

It's not what you know, it's who you know.

...thanks Mum.

Keeping in touch, dropping a card, sending an e-mail. It's not hard. But, so often, people tell me: *'Oh, I wish I was better at keeping in touch. I'm useless at networking.'*

Well, you're missing out. Keeping in touch and networking is crucial. They say you network in the firm's time and gossip in your own time. Whatever, make a contact and keep it.

As people move through their careers, progress, change direction, you never know how they might be helpful to you or you to them.

Keep in touch and have a free source of advice, information, fun, ideas and folk to feel good about. Is this exploitative? No, provided you understand that networking works both ways. You and your skills and talents have to be available, too.

In truth it has never been easier to keep in touch and have some creative, constructive gossip. There's e-mail, fax, phone, text and the handwritten note. Plenty of choice and no excuses.

So, how do you do it?

Here are ten tips for neat networking!

1   Set aside some time in the day or the week to network. Make a positive effort to keep in touch. Electronic diaries, time management systems and even the battered old Filofax make it easy. It need not be a long time. We're not talking half a day here. Invest just 90 seconds to rattle off an e-mail to a contact and say: *'You just came into my mind, how are you doing?'*

2   Make a list of the key people you want to keep in touch with and find reasons for doing it. If you are reading a newspaper and come across a news item or an article that would interest them, rip it out and send it to them. Scribble a note and say: *'I came across this and thought it would interest you.'*

3   Be spontaneous. If you think of someone, contact them. Don't wait, don't put it off. Pick up the phone and give them a call. Do it right now. Whilst you are reading this someone will pop into your mind. Call them and say: *'Hey, I'm reading this great management book by Roy Lilley. I'm into the bit about networking and you popped into my mind. He says spontaneity is the fun part of keeping in touch – how are you doing?'*

4   Keep your door open. Be generous with your time and expertise. Networking is a two-way thing. One-way networking is exploitation. Make it clear to people: *'I hope we can stay in touch. And if you ever need any information on the XYZ thing, you know, that's what I do and you only have to ask. If I can help, I will.'*

5   Never forget the power of the handwritten note. As we come to rely more and more on electronic methods of keeping in touch, communication, networking and good old gossip become invisible in the electronic blizzard of texts, e-mails, messaging and voicemails. A handwritten note stands out, makes a difference and gets noticed. Keep a few blank cards in the drawer in the office or tucked into your briefcase. Be ready and make a rule to send one handwritten note a week.

6   See above and carry a few stamps! Buy a book of stamps. The new ones are self-adhesive and come in a credit card-size folder. Be ready with the stamps to send a card, a note, a billet-doux.

7   In a room of people? Make it a rule, always, to say hello to at least five strangers. No good with strangers? Of course you are. Just go up to the most interesting looking and say: *'Hello, I'm no good with strangers but I guess there is no point coming to things like this if we don't take the opportunity to meet people. So, I picked you because you look interesting. My name's Gladys and I work... How about you?'* I promise you a friend for life! Or your money back!

8   Accept invitations. At the end of the day the last thing you may want to do is to go to a 'drinks thing'. Go. Make a pact with yourself. Stay half an hour and that's all. You never know...

9 Join a professional organisation, an out-of-work group or a club. Great places to network and make contacts.

10 Keep a record of the names of spouses, children, pets and places they go on holiday. Keep a record and use it next time you meet. If you show an interest in them, they will show an interest in you. Don't be disappointed if they are not as good at it as you are. That's because you are a professional networker!

Networking is an investment, friendship is fun and spontaneity is the key. So keep in touch and drop me an e-mail from www.roylilley.co.uk or roylilley@compuserve.com!

Next letter, please.

Five per cent of people think.
Ten per cent of the people think they think,
and the other 85 per cent would rather die than think.

Thomas Edison

OPPORTUNITY

opportunity n. **1** *a good chance* **2** *a chance or opening offered by circumstances*

I hate those annoying management-speak guru people who talk about every disaster being an opportunity. View everything as an opportunity, they say. I could stab 'em.

At least, I could have. I discovered something that changed my life and has stuck with me for years. I was never much of a success at school. In fact I hated the place. The smell of the polish, the miserable teachers. I think I was something of a loner.

I survived school by taking an interest in drama and sport. It was the sport that was to be my undoing.

We didn't do athletics, we did 'running'. Soccer was football and gym was circuit training. We turned up, did our stuff, got changed and went home. No warming up, stretching, warming down, strength exercises or nutritional advice. We may, occasionally, have had a bit of a thrash in the nets, or slam-dunked a few basketballs (just to show off to the girls' school across the road), but training and preparing was something we never knew about.

> I hate those annoying management-speak guru people who talk about every disaster being an opportunity. View everything as an opportunity, they say. I could stab 'em.

As a consequence, the onset of middle age brought with it damaged toe joints from ill-fitting footie-boots, tennis elbow from unsprung wooden rackets and a lower back wrecked from too much rotation and not enough warming up and warming down.

The result: a lot of back pain and a surgeon very willing to have a bit of a dig around the discs in my lower back. The upshot of all that is – a lot of back pain, still!

But there was a lesson. Whilst in hospital recovering from the first operation, I was told I could either lay flat or stand up, but I wasn't to sit – for ten days. I found it difficult to see this advice as an opportunity!

My incarceration at the hands of the health service coincided with my taking delivery of a very early laptop computer. The thing was the size of several house bricks and weighed nearly as much. It had a battery that lasted just long enough to boot the thing up and a processor that took three weeks to decide what to do. The screen was black and white!

Nevertheless, I was the envy of everyone. Relatives, doctors, nurses, administrators paid me cursory visits as an excuse to play with the leading edge of technology. I was stuck. Trapped. Nothing to do. Backache, a physio trained by the Gestapo, and food that was great when it was cooked but did not survive the nine-mile trolley ride from the kitchens, located, presumably, in the next county. And only the ceiling to look at.

Grim. At least it was. Very grim, until someone uttered the immortal words that drive me barmy. 'Why not,' they said, 'see this as an opportunity and use your newfangled thingamajig to write a book?'

'I can't sit down,' I said.

They pointed out that my techno-brick could be used standing up. The rest, as they say, is history. It got me writing and I've never stopped. The long suffering British public have been ranted at in columns, bludgeoned in books and poked fun at in scripts. Over 20 books and miles of column inches in magazines and newspapers.

It was an opportunity. Stuck in hospital, a laptop and all the time in the world to think, research and write.

I guess the truth is: we don't see opportunities because we don't look for them. When someone says 'look for the opportunity', it might just be worth putting the knife down, taking a step back and thinking about it.

Managers are the worst people I have ever met at seeing opportunities. I know, it is a foul calumny to pronounce on the whole of the management classes! But I find it is true. Not because managers are stupid, or can't make the best of a situation, but because they live in a vertical world. A world where lines of responsibility are defined and a hierarchy established. To see an opportunity often takes a sideways look. To turn a disaster into an opportunity is very difficult if you are crisis-managing the problem in the first place.

There is a management guru, whose name escapes me. I once heard him speak on the subject of opportunism. It was one of those 'when disaster strikes, turn it into an opportunity' presentations. I can't think why I ever went along.

Anyway, he said, when the bureaucracy and the in-tray are weighing you down, marinate yourself in it. Think how boring it is. Then switch your thinking to fresh flowers, green fields and the shape of distant mountains. The next thought that comes into your head should be an opportunity.

What an idiot. At least I thought he was an idiot. Do you know what? It works! Well it does for me – give it a try.

I wish I could remember the guy's name! I should thank him.

It also takes discipline and practice. If you really want to come up with an opportunity, then you must give yourself time and make yourself think.

Here's an idea that you can try alone or with colleagues. Find some space in your diary, block it out and call it opportunity time.

Review two or three things that have not gone so well and make a real effort to think how the outcomes might be seen as an opportunity. Not how you can learn from them, but how you can turn them into an opportunity.

WHAT ABOUT THE WORKERS!

What about opportunities for those working for you or with you? When did you last give them an opportunity? An opportunity to stand in for you, to make a presentation, to go on a course or run a new project. Opportunity givers soon find themselves opportunity makers.

When did you last ask the boss to give you the opportunity to do something, achieve something, or improve something?

And if they keep saying 'no'? See it as an opportunity to find another job! Next letter, please!

I never give them hell, I just tell the truth, and they think it is hell!

Harry S Trueman

P

PEOPLE

people n.&v. *1 persons composing a community, tribe, race, nation **2** a group of persons of a specified kind **3** subjects, a retinue, etc.*

How's your tribe? The folks that you work with and the ones that work for you? Can you remember what life was like when you were a foot-soldier? All those stupid orders, memos, direction and things to do? Bad tempered bosses, unrealistic deadlines and the grind of it all. How did you survive? Well, you didn't – you got promoted!

It is easy to forget what it is like to be at the sharp end. Nose to the grindstone and back to the wheel. (*Just try working in that position – Ed.*) What are you like to work for? What is your organisation like to work for? Do you know?

Just before Easter in 2002 *The Sunday Times* produced a supplement called 'The Best 100 Companies To Work For'. It made fascinating reading. Fascinating not just because of the unexpected companies that found themselves at the top of the list, but because of the reasons why they were at the top. The relationships they had with their staff – their tribe. They way they treated their people.

The top five companies were:

Asda	Supermarkets	HQ in Leeds
Microsoft	Computer software	Reading
Richer Sounds	Hi-fi retailer	London
Bain & Company	Management consultants	London
AIT	Computer consultants	Henley-on-Thames

The complete list is too long for this chapter, but it included the well known and the not so well known. Here are a few you will have heard of.

	Ranking
Bacardi Martini	9
SAP	11
Gore-Tex	16
Nationwide	23
VW	30
Astra-Zeneca	46
KPMG	82
Pizza Express	85
Tesco	100

In the top 100 there were a range of companies, from all over the UK.

IT companies did not predominate. For example, if you've ever been to a conference in Harrogate, you are sure to have been to the fantastic Betty's Café Tea Rooms. They came 20th! A shoe repairer and key cutting company called Timpson were sixth.

Not all the winners were big companies. Some employed over 100 000 and some just a couple of hundred. Some were public and others privately owned, some global and others, probably, in a town near you!

There does not appear to be any commonality in their size, shape or purpose.

Fancy entering your place next year? Send a short nomination letter (no more than 2 pages) to 100bestcompanies@sunday-times.co.uk

So, what made 'em great places to work? Some of the staff were very highly paid, others around the minimum wage. Some were in fashionable jobs, such as the media (Capital Radio) and others in law (Eversheds, solicitors). Supermarkets, department stores, nappy manufacturers and car insurance. No rhyme nor reason. What does this prove?

It proves this:

> Any company can be a great company to work for! Size doesn't matter!

Make a note and have a long hard think about this!

Here are some quotes and ideas from companies and their employees about what made them great places for people to work:

- When Wal-Mart took over Asda, the staff in each of the UK stores were invited to nominate one member of staff to fly to Arkansas, USA, to attend the Wal-Mart annual meeting and get a feel for the new owners.
- Six months ago, in response to staff requests, Asda introduced private medical care to cover male cancer and 'well-woman' cover.
- At Asda, older staff can take a 'Benidorm Break' – three months' unpaid leave in the winter – and their jobs are kept open until they return.
- Staff at Asda are given points if they sell slow-moving lines. The winner gets the keys to a Jaguar motor car for a month.
- Microsoft avoid 'sick building syndrome' by pumping new air into the entire building eight times an hour.
- Microsoft encourage workers not to stay too long in the office. Their 9 to 5.30 club donates 10p to the NSPCC each time they go home *before* 5.30 pm. Last year Microsoft raised £250 000 for the NSPCC.
- Everyone at Microsoft is on flexitime and more than half of the staff work from home. Managers' pay is tied to how well they manage to balance staff's work and home life.
- Microsoft encourage 'family outings' to the office with subsidised canteen, free ice cream and the loan of picnic blankets for use in the company grounds. There are external heaters for use in the winter.
- Microsoft staff can shop online and have the goods delivered to the office.
- Ninety-four per cent of Microsoft staff said 'work was fun'.
- In the reception area at Richer Sounds there is a parrot and two life-size models of the Blues Brothers.
- Richer Sounds staff have the free loan of holiday homes in St Tropez and Pevensey Bay.
- If staff work late at Richer Sounds they have free beer and pizza.
- Richer Sounds give 5% of their profits to charity.
- Bain & Company, management consultants, allow their staff 30 minutes a week to go and read to children.
- Bain & Company staff do work long hours, but it is monitored and targeted at no more than 55 hours a week. Anything over 65 hours is frowned upon and can trigger the manager's pay evaluation.
- At any time, up to 15% of Bain & Company staff can be away from work, running a charity, or a marathon, or seeing their family.
- Timpson, shoe repairers and key cutters, give staff grants for school football teams and charity work.

- At Timpson, staff are cared for pastorally as well as financially with free loans to help workers in debt and counselling services for family problems.
- Cisco, the Internet networking company, have had difficult times and have made 5000 staff redundant this year. Nevertheless, 88% of staff said the management genuinely sought their suggestions and made them feel part of a winning team.
- At Cisco, the company match charitable donations up to £700.
- At Bacardi Martini, all staff are entitled to a free three-course lunch and 24-hour use of the on-site gym.
- The insurers JTL have a bonus scheme to compensate employees' families when work infringes on home life.
- JTL offer a flexible benefit scheme giving options such as medical insurance and holidays to be bought or sold with the equivalent of cash.
- JTL staff may do 35 hours' paid voluntary work annually, partnering a nearby school.
- At Gore-Tex there is no standard management hierarchy. Staff work in teams of ten, led by whomsoever they decide, and salary is awarded by each team member anonymously ranking colleagues on their contribution to the team.
- At Gore-Tex, if a project fails, the team is taken out for a celebratory drink to reward them for trying.
- Bettys & Taylors' provide staff with free chiropody services, reflexology and health club membership.
- At B&T's, staff and managers have a two-way evaluation – every six months.
- Benfield's the insurers have TV sets on every floor, where staff can watch events such as Wimbledon.
- There are free yoga and T'ai Chi sessions at Benfield's.
- Capital Radio give free CDs to staff.
- Churchill Insurance give staff the chance to nominate a colleague for a 'Wow' award for outstanding performance.
- Nationwide, the building society, offer an employee-of-the-year award with a cash prize and a year spent as the company ambassador.
- At Anritsu, the Japanese telecom manufacturer, their mission statement says: *'Wholehearted and sincere dedication to ourselves and others, to our work, to our customers and society as a whole.'* This includes fairness, paying taxes, employment stability, fair competition, maintaining peace and security in society and respecting the spirit of each country's laws.
- The car breakdown service, Modial Assistance, celebrate births with a free 'baby box', staff are given £30 in luncheon vouchers each month and each Christmas a £50 voucher.

- VW, the car manufacturer, parks an ice-cream van in the car park in the summer and rented an entire cinema for employees and their families to see Harry Potter.
- Pret A Manger, the sandwich retailer, provide mothers-to-be with £20 towards maternity jeans and childcare vouchers at birth. On their return to work they are given health spa vouchers.
- Pret A Manger head office staff have to work in a retail outlet four times a year.

So, what's it like over at your place? Does this list make you want to change your job? Improve the one you've got? Or stop and think...

All these companies, small and large, really, really do think about staff needs and engage them in creative and productive ways.

If you are a waitress in a restaurant, chiropody services sound like a great idea. If you are a young family man, spending time at home is good news. Rewards are not free. Some of them are lavish but others are simple. Suggestion schemes that managers *do* listen to, make staff feel valued. Head office bosses that come and work on the shop floor make an impression.

Family values, charitable giving and involvement in ideas and decision making are the recurring themes. This is an excellent piece of research and well worth reading. Try *The Sunday Times* website (www.sunday-times.co.uk).

WHAT IS NEEDED NOW IS SOME THOUGHT.
SO WHAT ARE YOU WAITING FOR?

List ten ways to make people feel engaged, motivated, rewarded and part of the family and community.

Stuck? Ask the staff!

1
2
3
4
5
6
7
8
9
10

OK? Pick a letter...

The key to successful leadership today is influence, not authority.

Kenneth Blanchard

Q

QUERY

query n.&v. *1 a question esp. expressing doubt 2 a question mark 3 dispute the accuracy of*

Here's another one of those great sayings that you hear someplace and spend the rest of your life wondering who said it. In case the author of the phrase is reading this book – sorry! Give me a call and let me know so that I can reference you next time!

It really is one of those 'rip it out and stick it on the fridge with one of those funny magnet things'. Be my guest:

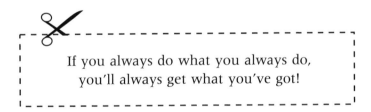

> If you always do what you always do,
> you'll always get what you've got!

Neat little aphorism, isn't it? Says it all really. If you're happy with what you've got, good luck. Go on to the next letter. If you are not – stick with this for a bit longer.

The famous comedian, writer, musician and actor, Danny Kaye, recorded the Hans Christian Andersen song about the King's new clothes. In case you missed it, it is about some sharp ex-double glazing salesman who sells the King an empty Sketchley's coat-hanger, claiming it is really an Armani suit; fools cannot see it but a wise man can.

The King, who is an egomaniac, saw only the Armani, 'put it on' and walked, naked, down the high street. The toadying citizens all say what a great *whistle-and-flute*. Everyone, with the exception of a little lad who blurts out: 'Mum, why is the King stark naked?'

Well, that's a sort of updated, loose synopsis. But you get the picture! The point of the story is this; it is only the naivety of the little lad that allows him to ask the important question.

What questions do you ask? Do you get in the right frame of mind? Are you prepared to challenge the *status quo*? Yes, sometimes it takes courage.

There is a neat little book by a change management guru (another one), James Champy, called *Reengineering Management*.* In it he coins the phrase 'living the question'. He describes the state of mind you need to get into.

✍	Got your mind right? ✔
A mind perpetually ready to revolt against its own conclusions.	
A mind prepared not for disbelief but for a constant, graceful scepticism.	
A mind that is open to any possibility, including impossibility.	
A mind of democratic hospitality to other views.	
A mind that is profoundly questioning, but buoyantly hopeful.	
A mind willing and able to bring established processes, procedures and people to judgement.	
A mind easy in the conviction that the verdict on any course of action is brought in, finally, not by science, not by reason, not by technology, not even by public opinion, but by results.	
A mind that can bear the light of a new day.	

I think this is a real neat list. It is a book well worth a read, particularly if you are involved with, or managing, change.

Champy invites us to 'live' four questions:

- What is the organisation for?
- What kind of culture do we want?
- How do we do our work?
- What kind of people do we want to work with?

* Champy J (1996) *Reengineering Management*. HarperBusiness, New York.

He says they have to be 'lived' simultaneously but presents them in an order of priority.

 Exercise

Think about the big questions and turn them into some smaller ones. For example, *What is the organisation for?* This is all about purpose. Here are some of the questions you might ask.

- What are we aiming at?
- What is the point of this?
- Who is this really for?
- What is the 'market'?
- Who is the 'customer'?
- What 'business' are we really in?
- Should we be doing this/all of this/some of this?
- If we didn't do this would we have to be invented?

Then use the questions as 'brainstormers' with colleagues in your department or organisation to define your purpose.

Now try the same exercise with the remaining three questions.

- What kind of culture do we want?
- How do we do our work?
- What kind of people do we want to work with?

Being prepared to query the *status quo* needn't make you a troublemaker or one of the awkward squad. Don't be tedious or have a glued focus. Being prepared to query is a creative way of challenging the organisation and moving it on. Doubtful? Well, read this:

> The key challenge facing us in the 90s is the same one that faces us every day: to keep taking the risk of change. Sometimes, when you are trying to improve, you break something that's already fixed. But unless you change and take the risk of failure, you limit your opportunities for success. That's why questioning, probing and reinventing are so important.
>
> *Leslie Wexner, founder chairman and CEO of*
> *'The Limited', Inc – another guru!*

Still not sure? Try this:

> Why do we go on dragging around this corpse of memory?

> *Emerson*

And what about this:

> It seems to be a rule of wisdom never to rely on memory alone, but to bring the past to judgement into the thousand-eyed present and live ever in the light of a new day.

> *Emerson – again!*

Still not sure? OK, I give up – go on to the next letter!

A leader is best... when people barely know he exists, when his work is done, his aim fulfilled, they will say, we did it ourselves.

Lao Tzu

RELATIVES

relatives n. *1 mutual relations, family members, blood relations*

In another part of this book – **T** for time management – I say this:

> Are you taking work home? Make a deal with the family: trade two evenings' work for a family treat at the weekend, or take the other half to the pictures once a week.

And this...

> You wouldn't miss a business meeting or let down colleagues by promising to speak at a meeting and not turning up. Treat your family commitments like business appointments – keep them!

And this...

 Tip

Should you be spending more time with your family? Got kids and never see them? Here's what you do. Figure out how many Saturdays there are between now and when the oldest child is 16. So, if you have a four-year-old, that's 12 years before they are 16. In 12 years there will be, give or take, 624 Saturdays. Next time you go shopping, buy a bag of dried lentils, count out 624 and put them in a jar. Keep the jar on your desk and every week take out one lentil and eat it. (It'll do you good!)

Watch the jar empty and see, right in front of you, what you are missing. How time is running out. So, what are you going to do about it?

No apologies for saying it again. How many relationships get busted by ambition? Is it worth it?

Have a long think and make an 'in-action plan' before you go on to the next letter.

One of the true tests of leadership is the ability to recognise a problem
before it becomes an emergency.

Arnold Glasgow

SEE OUTSIDE THE BOX

see outside the box colloquial. *1 concerned with recognising what can be learned by the study or observation of professions or situations other than one's own 2 reflecting practice or experience from outside 3 not being constrained for solutions to problems by custom and practice 4 stepping back from a problem, to seek a solution*

What problems have you got? Staffing, resource, timing, scheduling, people – you name it. Do you think you are the only one? I bet you are not. Running a hotel is like running parts of a hospital. Running an administration in the railway industry is like doing it in parts of the airline business. The freight business is about fleet maintenance.

Some years ago businesses managed to whip themselves into a froth of anxiety about the so-called Millennium Bug. At the turn of the year 2000 our computer systems were supposed to turn to jelly, switch themselves off and the world grind to a halt.

It was a universal problem. Who was the first to identify it as a potential doomsday scenario? Not the computer press! It was a far-sighted journalist writing in one of the trade magazines for the civil engineering profession. He had figured out that unless someone did something about the date switch-over, heating and cooling plants wouldn't work and lifts would get stuck halfway between floors.

These systems knew when they needed to be serviced and as part of a very smart risk-management programme, if they had not been serviced at the appropriate time, they shut down, for safety's sake.

The rest, as they say, is history. The world didn't grind to a halt. Aeroplanes didn't fall out of the sky and deep freezers stayed frozen. Thousands of computer anorak types sorted the problem. On the way to righteousness and glory they made a few quid for themselves and good luck.

The important part of the story is that, unless you happened to be a civil engineer, you wouldn't have known anything about it. The issue would have been spotted outside your box.

Working hard, obsessed by the day-to-day? Sometimes it is hard to step back, to be able to see the wood for the trees. It is possible to become so focused that you don't see anything at all.

✍ Exercise

Think about the work that you do. Not as a whole, but in components. List those components and then make another list of other professions and jobs where there is a similarity:

1 I talk to the public	1 Sales, retailing
2	2
3	3
4	4
5	5

OK, got your list? Now make a beeline for a decent-size newsagent and buy a magazine that deals with one of the jobs, or professions, you have listed on the right-hand side of the page. Stand by to be amazed that there will be articles and news items that deal with a problem in their world that you are trying to solve in yours!

Now you won't feel so lonely! More importantly, look at the solutions they are suggesting. Leaf through the small ads at the back. Look at the equipment they sell, look at the services they offer.

You'd guess that business gurus have a word for it! They do. It is commonality. Right across the business and service world – commonality. The bottom line is: we are all trying to do something for someone else. The methods vary but the end point stays the same.

Time for a **T**?

Outstanding leaders appeal to the hearts of their followers not their minds.

TIME MANAGEMENT

time management v. **1** *concerned with the best and most effective use of the time available by planning and evaluation of productiveness and work scheduling* **2** *individual responsibility for employing time productively and not wasting opportunity through lack of time*

Here are a few things that you can do with time:

- spend time
- do time
- waste time
- give time.

Yes, and you can idle time away. You can also work against time, work all the time, and do several things at the same time. You can be before your time and put up with things, for the time being. You can have a good time, hang on until half-time and have a bad time. You can avoid giving someone the time of day. Or you could lose no time passing the time of day. You can do a time-and-motion study on an activity that is time-consuming. How about defusing a time bomb, avoiding the time-fuse?

You might want to bury a time capsule, or take a photograph using a time exposure. Do you work in a time-honoured way? Are you a time-server? Are you having the time of your life in a time-share apartment in the sun, on holiday, in another time zone, forgetting about the time sheet and the time signal?

To keep your home warm you can set the heating by a time switch. You can watch a TV movie about intergalactic travellers, stuck in a time warp.

You could be a timekeeper, measuring the timeliness of work – on a timepiece and checking a timetable.

All that you can do with time. The one thing you cannot do with time is to make time. You can squeeze time and change your timings, but you cannot make it. Time cannot be fabricated or built. You can only organise your time. Here's a nice little aphorism. Cut it out and pin it to the front of your desk:

If you want something done, ask a busy person,
because they can organise their time to get things done.

The secret of time management is organisation. Pure and simple. There is no rocket science. It is all about getting organised.

For instance, do you keep a 'To Do' list? Does it look like this?

Ring Wendy

Do account figures for last quarter

Arrange for car to be serviced ✔

Make appointment with finance director re budgets

Write board report

Does your 'To Do' list help you get things done? No, of course not. Here's a tip. Write your 'To Do' list and then 'make the snake'. Snake? Yup. Leave the things on the list where they are. Don't cross them out, underline them or make a tick. Fill in a square next to the item and aim for a continuous line – make the snake. Like this:

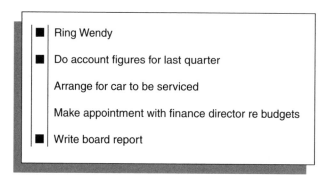

■ Ring Wendy

■ Do account figures for last quarter

Arrange for car to be serviced

Make appointment with finance director re budgets

■ Write board report

Why does it work? I don't know! The idea was given to me by a Harvard professor of business studies. He did it and suggested I tried it. I did and it works. Somehow things seem to get done. Making a solid line, or, as the professor called it, 'making the snake', invites effort. A 'To Do' list that is a muddle is for a person whose time is in a muddle. Try the snake!

Another tip he gave me was not to have separate lists for business, domestic, social or other purposes. Keep one list and keep it in front of you. That way you can see the whole picture.

Here are ten ideas to help you do twice the work in half the time:

1 FIND OUT WHAT YOU DO

Sounds stupid, doesn't it? You know what you do. You are a manager, doctor, nurse, finance person, salesman, accountant, planner, plumber, whatever. This is not about *what* you do. It is all about what you *do*! Do, in the sense of when and how much.

This is going to sound really tedious. I want you to audit what you do. In other words, keep a list. Don't groan and give up. This is important. I think if you keep a list of what you do, you'll be either proud of yourself, disgusted, amazed or embarrassed. Whatever it is, you need to know.

Here's what you do. Pick a typical day and keep a note of what you do. No such thing as a typical day? OK, keep a diary for a week.

Here's what it should look like:

	Activity			
Date:	**Phone**	**Meeting**	**Correspondence/e-mail**	**Etc.**
8.30 am				
9.00				
9.30				
10.00				
10.30				
11.00				
11.30				
Noon				

	Activity			
Date:	**Phone**	**Meeting**	**Correspondence/e-mail**	**Etc.**
12.30 pm				
1.00				
1.30				
Keep going until you finish the day				

The idea is to fill in the squares, roughly, with the amount of time you spend on each activity for every half-hour of the working day. You can make the intervals fifteen minutes if you work in that kind of a fast-flowing environment.

If you work at home, in the evenings, or weekends, make a table for that, too.

Too difficult? Not really. Lawyers and accountants do it all the time. They have to. Otherwise they wouldn't know who to bill their time to. Most of the 'consulting' professions keep an activity timesheet to enable them to send out one of those nice big bills, to each of their clients, detailing how much time they've spent on doing wonderful things for them. So, this is not rocket science, unusual, or weird. All you will be doing is to keep a record, for a couple of days, so that you can get a real feel for the amount of time you spend on your principal activities.

The next bit is for the really smart ones!

Now turn the data into one of those nice graphs that that nice Mr Gates makes it so easy to do in Microsoft PowerPoint.

Can't do the whizzy stuff? Learn! Ask the nearest fifteen-year-old. In the meantime, draw a graph. Aim for something like this:

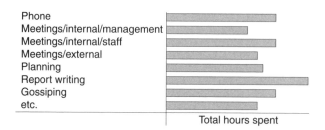

I have no idea what your graph will look like. But the question you must ask yourself is: do you want your graph to look like it does? Do you really want to spend that amount of time on the phone? Must you go to all those meetings? Do you really waste all that time going to the water-cooler and gossiping? Whatever! The conclusions may not be so obvious.

The idea is not to look for recriminations, blame or embarrassment. This is about having a good look at how you spend your time and deciding if that is how you want to go on investing the minutes of your working day.

Is there a better way? Can you get some of the stuff on the phone handled by other people, or should you spend more time on the phone? Do you need to have all those external meetings? Should you be looking for a way to spend more time with your staff? Can you jack up the time you spend in uninterrupted thought, planning and getting the next bright idea? Do you need to do a typing course, switch to a dictating machine, try voice-activated software or have more than one e-mail address, to help you prioritise? Should you spend more time at the water-cooler, finding out what's going on? Are you neglecting the folks at home?

Once you know what it is you *do*, you can figure out what you should be *doing*!

2 TREAT TIME AS MONEY

Why would you want to do that? Because time is money. Someone is paying you to do all this wonderful stuff and as far as they are concerned, your time is their money. However, take a few minutes to think about it slightly differently. Think about time in the sense of money. Money is valuable, finite and worth investing. So is time. Make a list of all the things you wouldn't want to do with your money:

- waste it
- neglect it
- fritter it away
- gamble with it, on losers
- spend it and get nothing for it.

Cross out the word money and insert the word 'time' and you'll see what I mean. If you made another list of all the things you wanted to do with your money, you could go through the same exercise. Money and time – it's easy to look at them in the same way. Time, really is money.

MEETINGS, %&**$ MEETINGS

Find yourself sucked into meetings that go on too long? Here's the answer.

Do a brief calculation of the total cost per working hour of all the individuals who attend the meeting. A rough estimate will do. Then write the answer on a big piece of paper and pin it to the wall:

These meetings are costing
£150 an hour.
So let's get on with it!

---

3 KNOW YOUR BODY CLOCK

I am one of those people who can work all night. Once I get in the groove I just like to keep going.

Over the years I've collaborated with a number of writers, to produce books on all sorts of management topics. Some of my co-authors have followed me into the small hours with no problems at all. Others have fallen over at midnight! However, I'm useless in the mornings. I can't think straight, can't get organised and never produce anything worthwhile. It is the way my body clock works.

Is it metabolism? Is it psychology? Who knows. What I do know is this: if I need to concentrate and get something done, any time before about 11 am is a waste of time. Anything after that and I'll stick it out until the task is finished.

So, when is your best time? Mornings, afternoons, evenings? Save the tricky tasks for the time you are at your best. Get the routine stuff out of the way and concentrate on the tasks that need to be right when you feel right. You'll get them done more efficiently, enjoy them more and get a greater sense of satisfaction.

4 LEARN TO SAY 'NO'

I once read a light-hearted article in a management magazine that likened us all to various breeds of dogs! It was very funny. Poodles, bulldogs, greyhounds – they were all there. Or should I say, we were all there! The

> Are you a pedigree, best of breed, thoroughbred spaniel?

comparison that really got me thinking was the spaniel.

Are you a spaniel? Willing, eager, enthusiastic, anxious to please? Of course you are. But are you too much of a spaniel? Do you take too much on? Is your in-tray bursting? Because you are good at what you do, do people take advantage? Are you nervous about letting go? Worried that someone else won't be able to do the job as well as you? Are you concerned about pleasing the boss, or colleagues?

Do you need to learn to say 'no'? Do you need to find the words that say: *'I really enjoy these kind of assignments, but I've got three others on the go at the moment and if I take on any more I could end up jeopardising all of them.'*

Do you need to learn the phrases that say: *'I really can't take on any more and do the job properly. What about giving it to Jenny? I know she is interested in having a go at one of these projects and I am very happy to keep an eye on her and help her if she gets stuck.'*

> Hiring staff? Don't be a spaniel. Hire someone better than you, stand back and take the credit. Hire someone worse than you and step forward and take the blame!

Learning to say 'no' is mature, sensible and grown-up.

5 DO THE WORST JOB FIRST

Got something lurking on your desk top that you've been putting off? Something in the in-tray that's been there since the days when you could buy a pint of beer for 1/9d?

Good time-managers don't let stuff fester. They do the jobs they hate – first. Get them out of the way. All the time you are doing the job you'll be thinking about moving on to the next job. And that'll be the one you like doing. Reward yourself. Give yourself something you like doing as a reward for getting the rotten job out of the way.

The job you least want to do is the job that will compost. By the time you get around to it, it will not only be a rotten job, it will be a rotten job with a ridiculous deadline and a boss breathing down your neck. That's no way to approach a rotten job.

The job you least want to do is the job you must do when you are fresh and looking forward to doing something else.

Polish it off – you'll feel better for it! Honest – or your money back!

6 Stay away from the Internet

I'm addicted. I can spend hours on the Internet. I can find out about the life cycle of the South American, lesser-spotted fruit fly, find the football results for the Italian league. I can search for quotes, derivations, origins, formulae, news, predictions, forecasts and prophecies. Book holidays, buy groceries and order the latest must-have whizzo gadget. I can waste hours on the Internet. I need to join Internetters Anonymous!

 **Hazard Warning**

The Internet is fabulous, inexhaustible and addictive. There is no finer, nobler and more enjoyable way of whiling away the working day!

However, if you must surf, there's a great website you must visit:

- www.ishouldbeworking.com

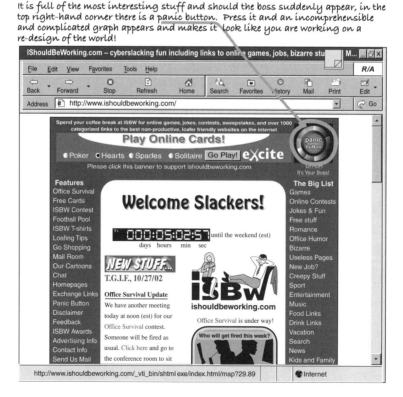

It is full of the most interesting stuff and should the boss suddenly appear, in the top right-hand corner there is a panic button. Press it and an incomprehensible and complicated graph appears and makes it look like you are working on a re-design of the world!

OK, that's enough time wasting – back to time management!

7 TRY NOT DOING MEETINGS, OR IF YOU HAVE TO, DO THEM BETTER

As I travel around talking with groups of managers and bosses, high on the list of 'moans' is the escalating amount of time spent in meetings.

My answer? Tough, you'd better get used to it! Meetings are not an add-on, not an interruption of the working day and not an appendage. Meetings are management.

Meetings are the inevitable consequence of shaping services around the needs of customers, clients and the people who provide the cash to pay our wages. Collaborating, merging, strategic alliances, developing products, inter-departmental liaison – all mean more meetings.

 Think about this

In a recent BT business survey, it was estimated that most European companies spend more on business travel than they do on advertising!

Planning meetings, brainstorming, progress meetings, outcome meetings, case conferences. Policy making, negotiating, settling disputes, trust building, managing change. Meetings about meetings!

What's the answer?

GET TOUGH AND GET INTO TECHNOLOGY

Do you know how much your meetings cost? That's the first step in getting tough.

Try my 'put the boot in' guide to making meetings work.

1 Work out how much it costs to hold a meeting. Time is as valuable as any other organisational asset. Calculate the cost per hour of holding a meeting, write it in big letters and pin it to the wall. Don't be embarrassed, just do it! Hammer home the cost of dealing with difficult people who dither, are indecisive, spend time on gossiping and tittle-tattle.

2 How many times have you been to a meeting and it's obvious someone hasn't read the agenda or done their homework? Make sure you never attend a meeting unprepared! Make it clear you've done your homework and don't have any truck with people who haven't. Don't be afraid to say: *'We are all busy people and I think we owe it to each other to do our*

homework – don't you?' Then fix the miscreant with your most winning smile! Bet they never turn up unprepared again!

3   Always insist that meetings start on time. Speak up, say: *'I think everyone knows we should get started at 3 pm and if we don't, I'm concerned that some of us will overrun into our next commitments.'* Be firm. Start on time, latecomers will soon get the hang of it. If they complain? Smile, say: *'I'm sorry but the start time is on the agenda and we all have other things to move onto.'* Or: *'We couldn't really wait around for you as we've not heard from your office that you would be late – we didn't know if you were delayed or not coming.'* And smile the dazzling smile only you can do!

4   Agenda – make sure there is one. No agenda? Don't waste your time. Meetings without agendas are like a journey into a jungle with no map. If the agenda is not set in advance, ask the chairperson: *'Before we start, shall we make a list of the items we need to cover?'* If you're really pressed for time think about asking for the agenda items that involve you to be taken together and then, when you're through, push off! Try and avoid 'any other business'. It's a gossip's charter. Do that in the car park, or over a cuppa before you start.

5   Always make sure the meeting runs to time. If you're in charge, make sure there is a big, conspicuous clock that everyone can see. Announce what time you intend to finish and keep an eye on the clock. It may mean cutting items short. Say: *'I'm looking at the clock and if we are to do justice to the rest of the agenda I think we are going to have to reach a conclusion on this item.'* If you are not in charge, be obvious in taking off your wristwatch, put it on the table and keep it in your eye line. Don't be afraid to say to whoever is running the meeting: *'I've got an eye on the time and I'm concerned that if we don't move on, we'll have items that we will not be able to do justice to.'*

6   Dopey chairperson? This is grim news. Try having a quiet word. Express your concerns about running to time or wasting time on gossip and chit-chat. If all else fails – grab the initiative and chair the meeting from the floor. Try phrases such as: *'Do you think we should move on?'* Or: *'This is interesting, but I think we should try and stick to the agenda, don't you?'* Don't forget the smile!

7   If there is a tricky or complex item to be discussed, don't wait for the meeting; get on the phone in advance and lobby for support. Take time to explain the detail and ask for backing. It speeds up the meeting and works a treat!

8   Do you really need to have a meeting? I mean really, really, really need to have one? Try to get a delegated authority from your group to deal with some issues with colleagues over the phone or by e-mail.

And technology?

Once glamorous options such as video-conferencing have now become routine. PCs with video cameras are cheap and can be linked, internally, using the network facility that comes with most Windows platforms since Windows '95.

 Tip

BT have a really useful service. Using your normal phone, BT can link endless phones, allowing you to have a virtual meeting without travelling.

Calls carry a small premium. BT will arrange to have the conference taped and provide itemised billing so costs can be identified and allocated. They also offer a translation service.

To find out more, call BT on 0800 778877. They can also link your PC for external video conferencing.

However, do you really need pictures? Try conference telephone calls. Internally, most phone systems have the capability. The only problem is, no one knows how to set it up! Make the IT department earn its keep – find out!

Think it might be too expensive? Look at the piece of paper you've pinned to the wall. How much an hour does a meeting cost you?

Meetings can be boring, dull, uninspiring, flat, slow, heavy, languid, fun, happy, a laugh, productive and just about everything in between. Don't overlook the role that the meeting environment can play.

Here are some simple rules that are often overlooked.

✍	Yup ✔
Does everyone know where the meeting is? Can they get to it easily? Do you need to send them a map?	
Is the time convenient for every-one? Take into account travel times and distances, other operational responsibilities, family and outside work commitments.	

	Yup ✔
Special access requirements to meet disability needs.	
Is the room well-lit and properly ventilated?	
Using visual aids – can everyone see the screen?	
Room layout – long tables are a no-no and hotel venues do it all the time. Round tables are better – insist on them.	
Does the timetable allow for plenty of pee/smoke/message-collecting breaks?	
Does everyone know who everyone is?	
Does everyone have to attend for the whole meeting? Hanging around till you get to 'your bit' is no fun if you can't play a part in the rest of the agenda.	
Can everyone see a clock?	
Is there an agenda and has it been published and circulated in good time?	

To meet or not to meet – that is the question. Here's the answer!

Time is wasted when a meeting's content is poor or when there is no obvious reason for people to have been dragged halfway across the territory for something that could have been achieved on the telephone.

Think of a meeting as nothing more than a management tool. Just like e-mail, fax, memos, phone calls and handwritten notes, meetings have a role to play. They are not the first line of defence or a knee-jerk reaction to a problem. Of all the communication mediums available, a meeting will be the most costly – use meetings wisely.

To meet or not to meet – your call:

Have a meeting if:	Don't waste everyone's time if:
You're the boss/leader/manager and there is an issue that you need advice or guidance to deal with	There is insufficient knowledge of the problem, or no data or information
There is a problem to solve or a decision to make and you want to involve a group in getting a grip on it. Especially if you need buy-in to implement a solution	The same result can be achieved by phone, e-mail or memo
Maybe no decision is needed but there is something that needs to be clarified, face to face	The meeting will deal with a burning issue, tempers are running high and there is a risk of a row. Use time to cool the group down and allow them to become more objective
You have a concern about an issue that you want to share with your group	The subject matter is highly confidential and a leak would be a disaster. Remember, there is no such thing as a secret
There is a cross-functional problem that needs a range of people to address it	The topic is trivial
There is confusion over lines of responsibility	You've already made up your mind about what to do. Don't turn your group into a difficult bunch by treating them as a rubber stamp
The group have indicated that they want to meet	It's about personal issues such as letting staff go, remuneration and individual performance. In the main, all that's best done one-to-one

Hazard Warning

Beware of 'regular meetings'. They invite routine and routine is the death of inspiration.

8 CREATE SOME SPACE

Create some space in your life. How do you do that? Get tough with yourself. You can create space by getting up fifteen minutes earlier and going through an exercise routine, or eating a proper breakfast. That'll make your mother happy!

You can create space by making sure you ring-fence some time for thinking or research. Create space by thinking about what you do. Go back to your time audit. Which bits do you want to swap, stop doing or be more efficient about?

Are you taking work home? Make a deal with the family: trade two evenings' work for a family treat at the weekend, or take the other half to the pictures once a week.

You wouldn't miss a business meeting or let down colleagues by promising to speak at a meeting and not turning up. Treat your family commitments like business appointments – keep them!

9 ORGANISE YOUR DESK

If you can't organise your desk, how can you organise your life? Have you got piles of stuff everywhere? Is your in-tray more like a compost heap? Have you got an in-tray, a pending tray, a hold-it-for-a-moment tray, do-it-later pile? Get rid of it all. Try and work with an in-tray and an out-tray. Pending doesn't help. In the same way that a carpenter looks after his tools, a painter prepares the wood and artists clean their brushes, your desk is part of the tools of your trade. Keeping it organised means you will work faster.

10 THE 90-SECOND RULE

What can you do in 90 seconds? Answer: more than you think! Ninety seconds gives you time to send an e-mail, write a letter, compose a memo, make a phone call, scribble a note, have a targeted discussion.

 Tip

Here's another tip from my friend the Harvard business professor and time management guru. Never refer to time in slabs of 5 minutes, 10 minutes, or even half an hour. Always say: *'I'll call you back in four minutes.'* Or try: *'This will take us eight minutes to resolve.'* Think about saying: *'I'll call you back in three days.'* Using 'odd' times does two things: it shows you value time and is unusual enough to be memorable for the other person. Silly, I know, but it really does work!

Don't leave stuff lying around. Use the 90-second rule to make a start – even if you can't get a job finished there and then.

Use 90 seconds to brainstorm a problem. Take off your wristwatch, put it on the desk and do a 90-second brain-dump on the most difficult problem you are facing. Scribble your thoughts down and use them as a basis for moving on. I bet you'll have trouble holding your breath for 90 seconds – but you can say a lot!

Got time for the next letter?

Failure is the only opportunity to begin again, intelligently.

Henry Ford

UNSUNG

unsung adj. *1 not celebrated 2 unknown*

When did you last go to the movies? OK, what about renting a DVD, or video? All right, enjoy a night in, feet up on the sofa, a pizza, a six-pack and a movie on the TV?

What do you like? Gripping yarns, cowboys, sci-fi, wars, romance? What about your favourite performances? Who is your favourite actor? Actress? Each year the industry celebrates its finest and best with the Oscars.

Whilst this book was being written the Oscar for the best movie went to *A Beautiful Mind*. The best actor was Denzel Washington and the best actress, Halle Berry. But you knew that. It made history and it was all over the news media.

I bet you don't know who got the award for the best screenplay.* Unless you are a real film buff, you won't know which film won the Oscar for the best sound editing.** Or the artist for the best original song.***

Can you imagine a movie without a screenplay? A movie with no sound?

These are the unsung heroes of the movie business. These are the people that make the difference and give us the movies to die for, the movies to cry for and the movies to stay on the couch for.

Dyaknowwhat? Every business, organisation and corner store has its unsung heroes. Everywhere there are Oscar winners. Allyagottado is find 'em.

Who is there, in your organisation that should get the Oscar for best supporting part? Who should take home the Oscar for technical support? Who is there that should have, on their mantelpiece, an Oscar for some backroom support, performance, assistance that has gone unsung?

---

*Julian Fellowes, for *Gosforth Park.*
** *Pearl Harbour.*
***Randy Newman, for 'If I Didn't Have You' from *Monsters, Inc.*

Somewhere in your organisation, there is a back that needs patting, a thank you to be said and a well done to be well recognised.

Go and find one, now. I'll wait...

 Done it? Good. Now, what about you? Have you had an Oscar? Your back patted? Someone said 'well done'? How do you feel? Like an Oscar winner? Or the Oscar polisher? Are you unsung?

I think there is only one person who can influence your morale. If you want to know who that is, stop reading, go to the washroom and look in the mirror. Your guide, motivator and mentor will be looking at you. The person who can pull you together, or take you apart, will be peering out at you.

But I also recognise that it is not always that easy. Pressures can mount, people can be difficult and personal confidence can ebb away. Any or all of this can undermine you and rob you of your self-esteem.

If you recognise any of that, we can put a stop to it right now. If you're OK, skip this bit and pick another letter! (Having first done the bit about Oscar winners!)

What you need is a life coach. For as little as $5000 a session you can have your own personal guru come and take care of you. In case $5000 is sounding slightly more than you can stretch to right now, there is another way. You can become your own life coach.

Here's how...

THERE ARE SEVEN STEPS

Step number one: Life coaches usually start by getting you to write a sort of a life history. Sounds dull? Well, I guess it depends on your life. Nevertheless, stick with me for a bit and let's find out.

Stick to the important events.

Turning points in my life have been ....

The things that mean most to me are ....

My successes are ....

What I really aspire to is ....

The most important lessons I have learned are ....

What really disappoints me the most is ....

So what do you know about yourself? Do you want money, love, admiration, to go back to school? Be specific. You want money? How much? You want a new relationship? Permanent or casual? You want to travel? Where?

Step number two: How much do you like yourself? Do you enjoy your own company? Can you spend a weekend with you? Do you talk to yourself and if you do, do you say nice things? Do you praise yourself? In other words, do you like you? Are you your own best friend? Do you give yourself a treat? Do you reward yourself? Do you treat you like you would a treasured and respected friend? Life coaches will tell you self-respect is at the heart of this. So answer the questions. Honestly, now!

I hate myself because ....

I like myself because ....

Step number three: Live for the here and now. Do you ever feel like you should be doing something else? Does your mind wander? Do you have trouble focusing and getting a job done? The trick is to focus, one hundred per cent, on the job in hand. That way you will become more productive and be pleased with more yourself – an essential ingredient in morale and self-image. Make a conscious effort to fix your attention on a particular job. Ignore the phone, resist the temptation to see what is in your e-mail inbox, don't join in the office gossip. Make a pact with yourself: 'For the next ten minutes I am going to focus exclusively on getting X, Y or Z done. After that I will reward myself with a coffee, gossip, phone call, whatever.' Start with small jobs and build up to bigger, longer and more complex tasks.

> ✍ I will focus on (..) task as my first
> experiment in living in the here and now.
>
> I will aim to focus for .... minutes.
>
> My reward will be ....

Step number four: Be more energetic. Easily said? Yup, I know. But if you are feeling low, the pile in the in-tray will get higher. The next thing is that you will focus on the stuff you are not doing. All feelings of achievement will disappear out of the window and the spiral of decline will make coming to work tomorrow a nightmare. So start with the basics:

- How much water do you drink? Go on, answer the question. The experts say you need to down two litres a day!
- How much booze do you drink? When did you last go a week without any alcohol?
- How healthy is your diet? Look in your fridge and be honest. All pre-prepared, frozen, microwave, salt saturated, calorific, sugar food of the devil?
- How fit are you? Do you take any exercise at all? Do you *ever* use the stairs instead of the lift?
- How much sleep are you getting?
- Can you relax, turn off and chill out?

The reason for these slightly threadbare, *life coach-y* type questions is that you never will be effective if you don't take care of yourself. If you are not effective you will know it and your self-esteem will take a dive. Energy drains away. So put a plug in the drain-hole.

> ## ✍ In the next thirty days I will re-energise my system by:
>
> Stopping this ....
>
> And, starting this ....
>
> I will reward myself by ....

Step number five: Put yourself in charge. Take the credit and take the blame. In other words, be responsible. It's easy to blame someone else, your education, the news, even the weather. If you do that you are not in charge. You will be what life coaches call 'voluntarily disempowered'. As the only person who can re-empower you is you, you can see you're stuck in a road you don't want to go down. It is very difficult to reverse out of this one. Of course, you cannot predict how life will treat you, or how people will react and deal with you. However, you do have control over how you will react.

This is a half-empty/half-full story. Two girls were born of a single mother, who was a hooker and an alcoholic. One daughter grew up to be just like her mother, with a string of broken relationships, unruly kids, no partner and living, in poverty, on a sink-estate. She said: 'What do you expect, with a background like mine?' The other daughter grew up to be a college professor, happily married and with a great family. She said: 'You don't think I wanted to end up like my mother, do you?'

 I agree, whatever happens, I will react to it in a way that does not disempower me ....

Step number six: See life in the round. Working hard and not getting anywhere? Myopic focus? Forgetting about everything else? Batteries need to be recharged, horizons widened, experiences need to be had. Life coaches use the word 'holistic'. Get the picture? The big picture!

For me, an holistic approach to my life would mean ....

I can achieve that by ....

Step number seven: Have a laugh! Having fun keeps you young, happier and healthy. Teach yourself to laugh at events. Yup, you have to take events seriously and not all jobs are a natural barrel of laughs, but make a point of seeing the funny side in something, every day.

So, feel better for that? Ready to award yourself an Oscar? When you're feeling unsung, give yourself a pat on the back, buy yourself a treat and prepare your acceptance speech!

Don't worry about the $5000.

OK, you gorgeous thing, pick a letter.

Consider how hard it is to change yourself and you'll understand what little chance you have of changing others.

Albert Einstein

VOLUNTEER

volunteer n.&v. *1 a person who voluntarily undertakes a task 2 make a voluntary offer of one's services for no payment*

Come on, just do it. You know there are hundreds of little organisations out there, trying to achieve something, do a bit of good, or just have some fun.

Volunteering is good for you. It broadens your experience, looks good on the CV and will extend and test your management skills. Let's face it. Getting the best out of staff is not the easiest thing in the world, but when push comes to shove you can push and shove! Working with volunteers is very different. No pushing and shoving. Just a lot of coaxing and motivation.

So, make time and develop yourself.

Make a start at:

- www.volunteering.org

or you could try the Association for Volunteering Administration and Volunteer Managers at:

- www.volunteeringinternation.org

Easier still, have a trawl through the local papers and see who is doing what.

Volunteering will extend you and you'll have fun, you might get fit, or develop new skills for nothing. Hey, and you'll meet a bunch of very nice people!

Next letter is **W**. D'ya volunteer for it?

You can hire people to work for you, but you have to win their hearts to have them work with you.

WACKY

wacky adj.&n. *1 crazy 2 a crazy person*

Let's face it, the world of work and management can be a very boring place.

Routine is the name of the game. The foundation of quality and quality services is 'process control'. How exciting is that? Actually, very! Well, for some... (Apologies to any quality anoraks reading this! I know that any day without major grief is exciting!)

> Quality is knowing what you want, making sure you get it, every time, until you don't want it any more. Very simple. And, it is important.

Where would McDonald's be were it not for the assurance that every time you walked into one of their restaurants you could rely on the fact that a Big Mac wouldn't look like a cheese and pickle sandwich and taste like a chicken biriani?

You wouldn't want to get on board an aeroplane piloted by someone who thought it might be a good idea to throw the rule book out of the window and display their cunning, stunt-flying routine.

The NHS is the same; who would want to be operated on by a surgeon who thinks it might be fun to see if it's possible to remove your appendix rectally?

There is no doubt about it; process control, routine, total systems management and operations procedures are there to standardise, leverage quality and meet expectations.

Is there room for anything else? Is there room for the unusual? Is there room for the different, the strange and the wacky?

Of course there is!

Tetley and PG Tips have been fighting a wacky war over the shape of a tea bag. A tea bag, for heaven's sake!

The world is facing environmental catastrophe, globalisation, famine, disaster and terrorism and the giants of the teapot industry are worried about the shape of a tea bag. Has the world gone mad?

Well, the answer is: yes and no! (*Don't let anyone say you sit on the fence, Roy! – Ed.*)

The T-boys are all thinking about market share. And they are not the only ones.

Whilst we talk about shopping trolleys below, what's the difference between a shopping trolley and a non-executive director?

Answer: A shopping trolley has a mind of its own, but you can get more food and drink into a non-executive director!

With apologies to non-execs everywhere, but we are giving ourselves permission to be wacky!

If you are still dumb enough to fiddle about, wasting time and treading water, shopping for bog-rolls, bath cleaner, furniture polish, washing-up liquid and tins of beans – piling them into a wire trolley and using up your Saturdays doing the shopping, instead of going to the movies, watching the game, shopping for interesting things to wear or plug in and play – then you will know, supermarkets are changing.

In the war of 'footfall', supermarkets are adding the strangest things to their inventory. In my local Tesco you can buy a bicycle, a fridge and a television.

Even more interesting is the fact that you can see an optician, have an eye test, buy a pair of glasses and choose from an extraordinary selection of sexy frames. You can have your prescription dispensed and before long, I predict, you will be able to see a doctor, or a nurse, or a health visitor.

OK, here's a question: would you have predicted any of this?

- Grocers who sell petrol.
- Petrol stations that are florists.
- Airlines that sell pensions.
- Record companies that sell booze.
- Estate agencies that are insurance firms.
- Telecom companies that rent videos.
- Underwear retailers who sell money.

- Film companies that are hoteliers.
- Insurers who are invisible.

No, of course you wouldn't. No one would. But it's logical and makes sense.

- The majority of supermarket shoppers arrive at the store with a car – let's sell them some petrol.
- Petrol station customers are predominantly men; put flowers in their face and they might just take a bunch home for their partner – a risky marketing decision that has been proved right. Petrol stations sell more flowers that florists!
- Virgin have a strong brand. They know their airline customers, for the most part, are in work, have an income, are intelligent enough to use the Internet to buy a ticket and have a strong confidence in the name Branson. So, what else can we sell them? When the pensions law was liberalised Sir Richard saw his chance and – bingo. He is now a major player in the pensions industry.
- Record companies that sell booze? Branson, again! He knows his market. Young people buy records. What else do they buy? Nights out, holidays and a round or two of drinks. Thus, Virgin Cola and Virgin Vodka.
- Telecom companies that rent videos? This is British Telecom. They have a pilot under evaluation. You can choose a video and have it piped down the telephone line to your TV. Sky use the same technology, as do NTL. If the customers have a telephone line – let's give them something to use it for.
- Can't think of a knickers shop that will lend you a few bob? Of course you can! Marks & Spencer will sell you some nice frilly things or some really dull Y-front things and give you a loan for some furniture, or to redecorate your house, or to consolidate your existing loans. They figure their customers are middle-class, have middle to above average incomes and are a good bet to repay a loan. So, let's sell them some money!
- Disney make films and they will make you very comfortable at one of their Disneyland hotels. Makes sense. Loadsa visitors in a year. Well, they might as well stay in our hotels.
- Invisible insurers? Who would have thought, even a few years ago, that you could buy insurance, over the phone, from a complete stranger? Buying insurance used to involve a trip to a broker, your best suit and suitably humble expression. 'Mr Broker, please find me an insurer.' Not any more. Lift the phone, get on the Internet, get the competitive quotes and that's it. You're insured in minutes. Technology has stuffed the insurance broker.

Wacky enough for you? You see, wacky isn't strange any more. The future is wacky, survival is wacky and staying in business is wacky. No barriers, no frontiers, no demarcations. Just a seamless flow of services that reflect customer need.

That's where we go from here. Into the world of the wacky.

We need the solid stuff, the organised stuff, the reliable stuff and the controlled stuff. But we also need anarchy, chaos, muddle and (yes) failure.

Ouch! Failure. There is a word we can do without decorating our CV!

If you haven't heard, read, or been told all the stories about Edison, you must have been living in a cave, or never been to school. We know that success is seeded in failure and determination. We know you can't invent a light-bulb without making a few lemons in the process.

It is OK to fail. Not fail in the sense of making a regular and total 'Horlics' of everything, I mean fail in the sense of having a go, trying something new and experimenting. Being wacky.

> Who would have been wacky enough to go to a planning meeting, worried about the price of petrol and suggesting that it would be a good idea to turn the forecourt into a florist? Would you? It takes courage to be wacky!

Quality is about replication. Innovation is about being wacky and taking risks. Double ouch...

Taking risks? Putting heads above the parapet? Taking a chance? You're damned right. I call it being wacky.

Wacky?

Wacky excites me. Wacky intrigues me. Wacky makes the world go around. Without wacky there would have been no man on the moon, no Kwik-Fit fitters, no Interflora, no Internet, no PalmPilot (incidentally, upon which most of this book was written), no seaside rock and no cats' eyes in the middle of the road. Most of the stuff we take for granted started out as a wacky idea.

So, where are you in the world of the wacky? Are you a starter-upper, an old hand or an outright sceptic?

We know about McDonald's. Each fry the same size and shape. We know about portion control and sachets of mayonnaise. But did you know it takes *exactly* 210 seconds to fry a portion of McDonald's chips? No, of course you didn't. Why should you?

McDonald's knew and they were happy with that. They knew how much fuel it takes to heat the oil, how much oil is needed and how often a chip gets burned. With that kind of management information they can do the sums, make the margins and predict the profits.

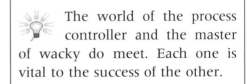 The world of the process controller and the master of wacky do meet. Each one is vital to the success of the other.

The safe world of quality enables them to introduce new products. Wacky products like the veggie-burger and the McFishy-things.

Enter some wacky person. Somebody thought it should be possible to make a McChip in 65 seconds – without cremating it!

This is a long story and the short answer is – they achieved it. Not much of an advance? Why would anyone want to bother with fiddling around with a chip-making process that has served McDonald's well since God had his first McNugget?

Think of it in terms of tonnes of chips, gallons of oil and kilojoules of energy costs. See what I mean? Wacky is not so stupid after all. Wacky saves money, time and raw materials.

How is it over at your place? Is it wacky? WACKY meaning: Willing to Attack Conventional Knowledge, Yes! Why not!

As opposed to: Won't Attempt Challenging Knowledge, You must be joking. . .

Can you pass the Wacky test? Try it on yourself and the people you work with. Ask them to rate the organisation, the department, any bit of it. . .

✎ **The Wacky Challenge**										
	Never									**Always**
	1	2	3	4	5	6	7	8	9	10
Willing to challenge the *status quo* and ready to think the unthinkable about new ideas, new systems and new services										
Accessible management, encourages staff to come forward with ideas – no matter how stupid they may seem at first										
Confident about its ability to understand customer need, change what is needed, to respond										

	Never									Always
	1	2	3	4	5	6	7	8	9	10
Knows that the pathway to improving what you do is not covered in smooth concrete, more like crazy paving, and accepts there will be a few slip-ups on the way. Where there are trips and stumbles, it doesn't turn it into the blame game and supports people when they fall										
Yearns to do things better. Really has a longing to improve. A craving to gain customer appreciation										
How's your score? Anything less than 60 and you're stuck in tacky – forget about wacky!										

How do you get to be wacky?

Some would say, if you have to ask the question – you'll never understand the answer! No, nothing is beyond you! Try this:

Virgin is great at selling records to the 16–35 year olds. They recognised that these customers have money to spend and a range of related needs, such as condoms, holidays, drinks and tickets. So they decided to provide them in the knowledge that the Virgin brand was strong, recognised and trusted.

Now it's your turn. Think about your organisation and fill in the blanks. Be prepared to change the questions slightly, to reflect where you work and what you do. The idea is to think about what else you could be doing, to support and delight your 'customers'.

Now fill in the blanks:

(Organisation) is great at .... We recognise
our service users have other needs, such as ....
We could provide ....
because ....

Want to have a wacky thinking session? Here's how.

There is a technique designed to help team-players get creative about problem solving. It's called *brainstorming*. Brainstorming is equally effective for finding good ideas and being wacky, both in groups and for individuals.

The process was first born of the management fads developed in the 1950s and works by separating the generation of ideas from the evaluation of how good they are.

The first step is to encourage a flow of ideas and the next step is to see if they are any good. It is very important that in the ideas generation stage, no idea, no matter how wacky, is trashed or criticised. The whole idea is to brain-dump ideas, thoughts and concepts. The wackier the better!

This is how it works:

- Set a fixed period of time to gather the ideas. Even if the group runs out of steam before the time is up, keep going and keep the group focused until the end of the period. Sometimes the best idea comes in the last five seconds.
- There must be *no* criticism of any idea, however tangential (or wacky) it may seem. Good ideas often come out of the wacky ones.
- Have someone write all the ideas down so everyone can see them, on a flip chart or white-wall, or some such.
- It's OK to build one idea on top of another one.

When time is up, evaluate the ideas against the following criteria:

- value/benefit
- cost
- feasibility
- resources available/needed.

 Exercise

Follow the rules and hold a 'brainstorming' session for a real-life issue you have over at your place. See if you can generate new and wacky ways of solving issues or creating ideas.

Write down some issues that you could 'brainstorm'.

Feeling wacky enough to try the next letter?

Power lasts ten years, influence not more than a hundred.

Korean proverb

X-RAY

x-ray n.&v. *1 electromagnetic radiation of short wavelength able to pass through opaque bodies 2 an image made by the effect of x-rays*

Can you see through opaque bodies? No? Well, you can see over the top, around the side and underneath! What are we interested in seeing? The future, of course. Can we develop a Superman-style, x-ray vision to see into the future? You certainly can.

If you want to know what will happen in the future – have a look at the past. What goes around, comes around. Look backwards to see what's in the future. History has all the answers you need.

Want to know about the future of organisations? What will happen where you work? What is around the corner for you? Easy, I'll show you how to get started.

Think about life cycles. Think about birth to death. Beginning to end. There are five stages to think about:

- chaos
- infrastructure
- technical improvements
- realignment
- life and death.

CHAOS

All businesses are born into chaos. Someone has a good idea and there is a chaotic scramble to see if it works. The first motor car is a perfect example. Some bright spark made a motor and frightened everyone to death with the noise of the thing and had to employ some luckless soul to walk in front of it, waving a red flag. The car had nowhere to go. The car was stuck in the wheel ruts made by horse-drawn carriages. People laughed, the horses bolted and the guy with the red flag got run over. Chaos.

The railways were no better. The first railway train only travelled 20 feet. Why? Because that's all the railway track they had. It simply shuddered and huffed and puffed its way up and down a yard.

Aeroplanes were no better. People were determined to fly. Many died in the attempt. When they did manage to get a plane off the ground, it had poor controls and went down as quick as it went up. When the Wright brothers made their epic flight, everyone was very impressed at their daring but the plane had no purpose.

All very chaotic – what's next?

> Read these paragraphs and see the future. Think about the dotcom industry. Some would say dotbomb. They've gone broke as fast as they were formed.
>
> Folk have lost a fortune. Want to know the future for the dotcom industry? Read on, about the planes and trains and motor cars. . .

INFRASTRUCTURE

OK, let's get organised. When somebody built a road – the cars could go somewhere. When they got the hang of building a railroad, laying tracks and building railway stations – trains started to look like a good idea. Once they had a few runways and something that looked like an airport, people could travel. They were in business. A little infrastructure can do a lot for a good idea. End of the chaos period.

What's next?

> What will it take to turn a dotbomb into a dotsuccess? Infrastructure! Just like cars need roads, railways need tracks and aeroplanes need runways and terminals, so the dotcoms need infrastructure. They need their own road. It's called a superhighway. As more of us get access to the Web and the kit becomes more ubiquitous, so we will be more willing to buy goods and services from the Internet. Infrastructure is the Web's next step.

TECHNICAL IMPROVEMENTS

Build a faster car, a cheaper car, a bigger car and someone will say: 'Maybe a car is not such a bad idea – let's build one, too.' Technical improvements, spurred on by competition, create benefits realisation. People want cars. Now, we have seen, within the lifetime of a man, cars have gone from chaos to commuting. Huge technical improvements have made cars safer and more reliable.

> Still thinking about the Web? The big changes are just around the corner. Just like the boom in the vehicle industry was triggered by technical improvements leading to benefits realisation – so it will happen for the Internet and Web commerce. Access to e-mails and the Internet can now be achieved from a mobile telephone. Goods and service and secure payment methods are in the here and now. In the future we will buy our holidays, order our groceries and switch on the oven in our house, ready for our return, all from a telephone the size of a box of matches.
>
> The future can be seen by studying what has gone before.

And then?

REALIGNMENT

This is where it gets difficult. But that doesn't mean any the less predictable. Realignment means companies losing sight of what they are doing, or losing their grip on the day-to-day.

Think of it this way. Arguably the world's greatest retailer, Marks & Spencer, went through a period where they lost customers, lost profits and lost their way. They had followed their success by venturing into areas that were not part of their core business and they made life more difficult for themselves by extending their trading into other countries. M&S became a muddle to manage and had lost focus.

To survive they followed the well-trodden path of realignment. In other words, they went back to what they were good at.

Some companies realign differently. Pharmaceutical companies are fond of merging. Glaxo with Wellcome, Glaxo Wellcome with SmithKline

Beecham, Astra with Zeneca and so on. The pharma-world is complicated. To survive they need a favourable regulatory environment, plenty of money for research and development, and a pipeline of medicines that are of value to patients and healthcare systems. Sounds easy, doesn't it!

Pharma-companies get themselves into all sorts of messes and they try to realign their way out of trouble. They think that by merging they will leave their troubles behind. The only problem with that theory is that in practice it seems not to work. When companies merge, they leave behind one set of problems and pick up a bag full of new ones!

All studies of the bank mergers that took place in the sixties and seventies would seem to show that they didn't save any money, didn't improve shareholder value and did not reduce operating costs. Pharma-companies don't seem to be faring any better.

 Hazard Warning

In its quest to be businesslike, the NHS has followed the merger path in pursuit of efficiency.

Just like the world of business, they are finding they may dump a few problems but they soon pick up new ones, different ones and bigger ones. None of them seem to save any real money and none of them seem to be any more efficient. History repeats itself! Even in public services.

Realignment can sometimes be done well and to great effect. British Telecom appear to have achieved it by splitting out its new web-based services and mobile tele-terrific stuff to a new company called O_2 or some such. BT have a 92% market dominance in the traditional telephone, copper wire to the house business. However, they know the future is in wider bandwidth, faster transmission of data and more glamorous telecom-based services.

In order to get into that business they spent a fortune on buying licences and, in the process, gave themselves something of a problem.

They did the right thing. They recognised they were, essentially, managing two businesses. One in the realignment phase – the copper wire business – and one in the chaos sector – the O_2 web-based business. They split the two businesses – exactly the right decision! Well done BT! It takes very different management to run a chaos business than it does a realignment sector business.

And finally?

LIFE AND DEATH

This is the key phase. Survive this and you've cracked it. Well, for a while, anyway!

This is where you innovate or die.

The life and death phase is where outmoded businesses disintegrate. Manufacturers of gas lamps will know exactly what I mean. Thanks and goodbye.

For the insurance companies it was a critical phase. Do you remember the time when buying insurance meant visiting a broker and grovelling to try and find the best price? Not any more. Do you remember putting on your best suit and being very nice to a man who might be able to fix you up with a mortgage? Well, stuff that.

The insurers have innovated and now run their businesses from call centres. A few phone calls are all it takes to insure, reinsure and renew. You can even buy a pension over the phone, change your mortgage arrangements and insure the contents of your house.

Call centre technology is reinventing and saving businesses with high overheads. Banking, travel and holiday businesses are going down the same route.

Businesses are fragmenting to get bigger. Remodelling using technology platforms that bring them close to going full circle – back to the chaos section!

So what goes around comes around:

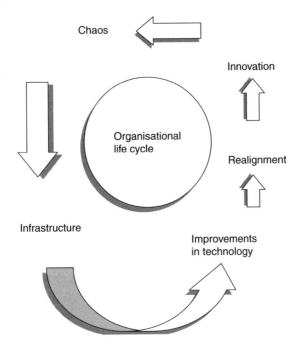

WHERE ARE YOU?

Can you see your future by looking at the past? Which part of the cycle are you in? Where do you fit into the circle? What other organisations can you study to get a feel of what the future might hold for you?

 Exercise

Describe the part of the cycle that your organisation is in and plot the future. Don't worry about the time lines. Start by identifying your present location and thinking what is likely to come next.

Then think about some companies or organisations that have gone through similar parts of the cycle. What happened to them?

Finally, try and fix a time line.

That's it. Welcome to the future! Do you like what you see?

Fancy the next letter? **Y** not?

People ask the difference between a leader and a boss;
the leader leads, and the boss drives.

Theodore Roosevelt

YAMAHA

Yamaha n. *1 Japan-based, international, industrial manufacturer, broadly founded across technology, automotive, engineering and entertainment sectors*

Why Yamaha? Well, it is a story of corporate failure that should have been a spectacular success. There are lessons to learn, comparisons to make and thoughts to be thunk!

Yamaha is a good **Y**, but in the context of my personal management alphabet, there is only, sadly, room to cover the top line of the story. Looking at how other people succeed and fail is an essential part of our own success and failure.

The Yamaha story is about a battle. Known as the H–Y War, it is the corporate battle for market share between two very similar organisations. Honda and Yamaha – a bare knuckle fight.

The story begins back in the 1980s. Yamaha had had enough of Honda's market dominance, decided that the market for motorcycles was growing, and

 Tip

MBA students and management anoraks might like to know there is a book that gives you the real deal on this story. It is *Competing Against Time: how time-based competition is re-shaping global markets.** Don't be put off by the title! These gentlemen know a thing or two about corporate culture. They are both senior partners at the Boston Consulting Group. It is one of those books that management gurus often quote. Indeed the great guru of gurus, Tom Peters, devotes time to it in his own management tome, *Liberation Management*. Another must-read for the aspiring management mystic.

* Stalk G Jr and Hout TM (1990) *Competing Against Time: how time-based competition is re-shaping global markets.* Free Press, New York.

in 1981 they started work on a new manufacturing facility that would make them Japan's number one motorcycle manufacturer.

At that time Honda were busy making 60 different types of motorcycle models. Now, that is complicated. I mean involved, convoluted and very difficult. Just think of it in terms of parts, supply chain and inventory.

Honda recognised the challenge that the new Yamaha factory would mean to them and in the next year and a half, flooded the motorcycle market with 118 new models! Honda turned motorcycle manufacture into high fashion. *Haute couture.* In their book, Stalk and Hout say motorcycle manufacture was turned into a 'matter of fashion'.

Yamaha were stuck and surrendered the battle to Honda. Where did Yamaha go wrong? They had the foresight to see a market sector that was growing. They had the courage to make the decision to build, they had the money, they had smart people and they got on with it. Sometimes, that isn't enough.

Yamaha saw the market and manufacturing through today's eyes. Not tomorrow's. They built a factory along existing manufacturing lines. They thought making more of the same would do the job. Honda looked beyond function and thought fashion.

Honda saw the future very differently. Honda recognised they had to give people reasons to become customers. They knew that they could build motorcycles that would go on forever, their build quality is so good. Honda had to give people extra reasons to buy. Turning a motorcycle into a fashion item, by widening choice, revamping design and turning a *could-have* item into a *must-have* item, was the difference between gaining market share and not.

Honda are not the only ones to look beyond merely manufacturing a complicated product really well. Sony and Intel are both examples of the same thing. Nokia are another company that understand the 'fashion' trick. Mobile phones with different coloured covers, different display screens, personal ringing tones and all manner of 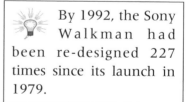 By 1992, the Sony Walkman had been re-designed 227 times since its launch in 1979.

accessories are now a must-have. Nokia have learned the trick of looking beyond function and into fashion. Forget the dull job of making a phone call, think fashion.

Toshiba, the laptop manufacturers, are another example. A new version of their laptop every three months tells its own story. The Volvo 400 series was launched with 88 different specification variations.

Why aren't all organisations like Honda and Sony and Toshiba and Intel and Nokia?

Back to Stalk and Hout for the answer. They argue that organisations are designed to 'soak up time'. Their research into company performance and behaviour helped them to develop a series of rules. Here is one of them:

> Most products and many services are actually receiving value for
> only .05 to 5% of the time they are in the value delivery system
> of their organisations.

Now, if you put that another way, it means that 95–95.95% of time is lost time. Honda beat Yamaha because they designed a delivery system that delivered flexibility and throughput in a faster turnaround envelope.

The gurus have an expression for it. It is called *cycle time compression*. In English? Well, it is not 'get the product or service through the processes faster'. This is not about sprinting or running faster. It means speeding up the whole service, or product delivery cycle. Tom Peters calls it 'hustle rather than speed'.

Jon Simpson, former president of Titeflex, is quoted in *Liberation Management*:

> The idea was to rebuild the company, a *blank page* approach. The
> key thing was flowcharting all the processes and at each step you
> ask, ten times: 'Does this add value for the customers?'

 The nineties will be a decade in a hurry, a nanosecond culture. There will only be two kinds of managers: the quick and the dead.

Dan Vice, Vice Chairman, Northern Telecom

So how does that leave you in the 2000s and beyond?

OK, all very anecdotal and interesting and guru-y but what does it mean for me, you and the places we work? Is Yamaha relevant to you?

I think the Yamaha and Honda story is very much about you and where you work. The relevance is about responding to customer need, it is about maintaining your place in the market and it is about survival. No matter if you work in the sexiest of lip-smackin', ace-tastin' super-thrilling, leading-edge places or the quiet backwater of a difficult public service. The message is the same:

If it don't add value, don't do it!

Yamaha's factory, although it cost millions, didn't add any value. It was Honda's fleetness of foot and their ability to compress their manufacturing cycle that added the value. It is the stupid, cheap and unbelievable press-on covers that add the value to the Nokia mobile phone.

You need to do a Jeremy Paxman – ask the question ten times. Does this add value for the customers?

Put another way, look at everything you do and ask: does this improve the customer experience?

Here's some white space – start the flow charts here!

Last letter coming up.

A good leader inspires others with confidence in him – a great leader inspires them with confidence in themselves.

Z

Zzzzzzzzzz

Zzzzz n.&v. *1 Onomatopoeic expression of sleep **2** algebra, the third unknown quantity*

I know, I know. You're thinking: sleep and the third unknown quantity? This is going to be some finish!

Let's start with sleep. Are you getting enough? The older you get, the less you need. Do I sound like your mother?

OK, joke over. Let's talk about sleep and unknown quantities.

More years ago than I care to remember, I found myself wandering around London's Waterloo Station at some ungodly hour in the morning. I had arrived on a boat-train (*What's that? – Ed.*), as far as I can remember, via France, from some place in Switzerland. There was a fair old wait until London woke up and the next train was ready to take me the rest of the journey to my home.

In those days Waterloo Station was not the café society, shopping arcade, wall-to-wall-pub place that it is now. It was cold, desolate and very miserable-looking. I decided to kill some time and go for a walk. I ventured out into Waterloo Road, turned right, walked for a while past the – now extinct – blue police box, beloved of *Dr Who* fans, crossed the road by the Union Jack Club, a hostel for servicemen and women, and past the green, wooden news vendor's hut. I found myself outside the Old Vic theatre.

At first I couldn't quite make out what it was, but as I got closer I realised there were 20 or so bundles, in the doorway and on the pavement alongside the walls of the theatre. The bundles turned out to be people, huddled to-gether, sleeping.

These days we don't notice bundles in the doorways of London and other big cities. To our everlasting shame, people sleeping rough have become part of the scenery. Politicians, policy, money and the Rough Sleepers Initiative have tried to make an impact on the problem. Nevertheless, men and women sleeping in doorways is still a common sight.

It is not only in Britain. I've seen it in Paris, Berlin, Barcelona, just about everywhere in Europe seems to have the same problem.

However, back whenever it was, when I was killing time and walking down the Waterloo Road, in London, at four in the morning, it was a very unusual sight.

I was curious and went for a closer look. For many of the bundles it was too cold and too uncomfortable to sleep. They were happy to talk.

Why were they there? They were queuing for tickets. Tickets to see *Hamlet*. Tickets to see Richard Burton playing Hamlet. They were fans. Burton's portrayal of Hamlet was legendary and they weren't going to miss a moment. They wanted to be first in the queue. They wanted to be sure of the best seats.

I wandered off and left them to freeze to the pavements. I had a sneaking admiration for them. I couldn't see me ever being that excited about anything.

Then I got thinking. How many actors know the words to *Hamlet*? How many actors could learn the words to *Hamlet*? How many actors are there that could stand on a stage and give a passable portrayal of Hamlet? How many actors are there that could stand on a stage and give a very good performance of Hamlet?

What's the answer? I have no idea, but I would guess hundreds. Maybe even thousands.

What was it about Richard Burton's Hamlet that would make middle-class, sane people freeze on the pavement? What did he have that the others didn't? What indefinable extra something did Burton have that put him at the top of his profession and made him worth sleeping on the streets for?

He had a magic. A charisma. A charm. He could cast a spell over his audience. He was hypnotically good. The voice, the movement, the menace. He had a depth of concentration that swept the audience, with him, into the world of Hamlet. He was goose-bump good.

So, here's the final question for the final letter of this highly personal, introspective, idiosyncratic take on the 26 most important topics for managers. Managers struggling to make the best of the challenges of the twenty-first century.

What do you do? How good are you at doing it? How good do you want to be at doing what you do? How hard are you going to try, to be the best at what you do?

Are you worth sleeping on the streets for?

ENDNOTE

Don't fancy my choice of alphabet?

Try this one instead:

- **Angry** – it's OK to get angry, but not in public and not too often. Better to let off a bit of private steam in the gym, or walking part of the way home.
- **Bravado** – you'll need a touch of this at times! What manager would admit, privately, in the dead of night, that it was bravado that saw them through a tough period?
- **Creep** – someone has to tell the boss how good you are. Bringing yourself to attention by doing good stuff is no bad thing.
- **Duck and dive** – who hasn't had to, on occasions?
- **Egoist** – if you don't believe in you, who does?
- **Fun** – sure, why not, have plenty of it and where there isn't any, invent some!
- **Grateful** – there will be an occasion, a moment and incident every week of your working life where you will be grateful to someone for something. Either a colleague who dug you out of the mire, or perhaps a teacher, mentor, instructor, or – heaven forfend – a guru who taught you something you put into action. Remember to say thank you. Drop them a note, an e-mail, just express gratitude. It's free!
- **Hate** – don't waste time on it. Move on.
- **Ignorance** – there's plenty of it about. Ignore it, exploit it or snuff it out by teaching. Your call.
- **Joke** – *see* fun!
- **Kaka** – it is a large New Zealand parrot. Try not to be one. Think for yourself.
- **Lust** – why not? It's a great motivator!
- **Magic** – find some, every day. Or, create some, for someone.
- **Neanderthal** – there are still some around, try not to be one!
- **Outrageous** – fantastically important that you can be. Practice, often!

- **Proud** – I don't think it's a sin. You've worked hard, done the right stuff, why shouldn't you be proud of your achievements?
- **Quit** – never do it. Never walk out of a meeting, slam down the phone or walk out of a job. A quitter never wins and a winner never quits.
- **Rude** – be sure to be it, all the time. Health I mean, rude health!
- **Stylish** – try and be. It's not about fashion or having a wardrobe the size of Posh and Becks'. Stylish is about you and how you behave.
- **Trouble** – try not to make it, but prepare for it, handle it and move on. Managers are all about troubleshooting and seeing trouble coming. If not, we would only need administrators and could save loadsa money on the salary bill.
- **U** – spend time on you. Spend time in uninterrupted thought, get some fresh air, think about what you eat. Be good to you.
- **Vain** – *see* U.
- **Wow** – find some, create some, look for some. If there is something to say 'wow' about there must be something going on!
- **Xerox** – the modern office equivalent of the parish pump. Visit often and gossip!
- **Yugoslavia** – think how lucky you are that you don't live in that part of the world. Enjoy life and don't waste a day.
- **Zebra** – the only thing worth seeing in black and white!

Still don't like my suggestions? OK, your turn:	
A	B
C	D
E	F
G	H
I	J
K	L
M	N
O	P
Q	R
S	T
U	V
W	X
Y	Z

They are your choice; no excuse for not following through!
   All the best!